The
God Dialogues:
A Philosophical Journey

Torin Alter

and

Robert J.

New York   Oxford
OXFORD UNIVERSITY PRESS
2011

Oxford University Press, Inc., publishes works that further Oxford University's
objective of excellence in research, scholarship, and education.

Oxford New York
Auckland Cape Town Dar es Salaam Hong Kong Karachi
Kuala Lumpur Madrid Melbourne Mexico City Nairobi
New Delhi Shanghai Taipei Toronto

With offices in
Argentina Austria Brazil Chile Czech Republic France Greece
Guatemala Hungary Italy Japan Poland Portugal Singapore
South Korea Switzerland Thailand Turkey Ukraine Vietnam

Published by Oxford University Press, Inc.
198 Madison Avenue, New York, New York 10016
http://www.oup.com

Oxford is a registered trademark of Oxford University Press

Library of Congress Cataloging-in-Publication Data

Alter, Torin Andrew, 1963–
The God dialogues : a philosophical journey / Torin Alter and Robert J. Howell.
p. cm.
Includes bibliographical references (p.) and index.
ISBN 978-0-19-539559-4
1. God (Christianity) 2. God—Proof. 3. Agnosticism. 4. Atheism. 5. Imaginary
conversations. I. Howell, Robert J. II. Title.
BT103.A47 2011
211—dc22
2010023203

Printing number: 9 8 7 6 5 4 3 2

Printed in the United States of America
on acid-free paper

For Janet B. Howell
and Dora and Irving Alter

Contents

Preface

Debates about the existence of God often collapse into heated battles in which ideology takes the fore and reason goes by the wayside. The topic can, however, provide fruitful opportunities for philosophical reflection. Such reflection has the potential to help us not only decide what to believe but also better understand why those who disagree with us believe as they do. It is in this spirit that we have written *The God Dialogues*, an extended debate among three friends on a post-graduation road trip from Boston to San Francisco. During their philosophical journey, the trio—an atheist, an agnostic, and a theist—discuss the relationship between God, morality, and the meaning of life; the rationality of theism; and the central arguments for and against God's existence.

We have tried to present all viewpoints accurately and fairly. But we have made no attempt to portray substantive issues as mere matters of opinion or to artificially create the impression that no viewpoint has the upper hand when this is not the case. When the evidence unequivocally supports a specific conclusion, that fact is acknowledged.

In the process of writing this book, we found ourselves examining our own beliefs from new angles, and we hope readers will have a similar experience. Rationally assessing one's religious convictions can be unsettling. But we believe doing so is an indispensible, or at least important, component of the examined life.

T. A & R. J. H

Acknowledgments

Many conversations and debates went into the creation of this book, and our debts are far reaching. We would like to thank in particular Janet Alter, Kevin Alter, Marion Alter, Irving Joseph Alter, Rick Asherson, Eric Barnes, Jonathan Benstead, Emily Brait, David J. Chalmers, Yishai Cohen, Alana Crowe, Chad Davis, Lanie DeLay, Chris Dodsworth, Jeremy Fantl, Joshua Ferris, Justin Fisher, Bryan Francis, Colleen Gerrard, Daniel Graf, Robert Gressis, Bill Hawk, Allan Hazlett, Mark Heller, H. Scott Hestevold, Amy Howell, Charles A. Howell III, Janet B. Howell, Lewis B. Howell, Robert J. Howell Sr., J. Gregory Keller, Jerome Kramer, Garrett Kyle, Clayton Littlejohn, Megan Marrin, Dana Maldonado, Luis Maldonado, Christina Mancuso, Robert Miller, Yujin Nagasawa, Derk Pereboom, Joshua Quick, Stuart Rachels, Nanette Sawyer, Houston Smit, Donald Smith, Elliot Sober, Billy Tate, John Wise, Chase Wrenn, and our students. We would also like to acknowledge the support of the philosophy departments of Southern Methodist University, The University of Alabama, and New York University.

1
Outside Boston

God, Value, and Meaning

Shortly after dawn, a black Honda Civic is idling outside of a university library. "Cali or Bust!" is written on the rear window, and two recent graduates, Gene Sesquois and Theodore Logan, are sitting in the front seats. Theo honks twice.

THEO: C'mon! Where is she? We have to hit Plymouth Rock by midday if we're going to keep to our schedule.

GENE: You know Eva. She's probably talking the ear off someone she met in a class freshman year.

THEO: Why did she have to stop by the library anyway? Does she really want to read on this trip? We just graduated! This is no time for reading!

GENE: It's not about reading. She's one of those people who doesn't feel ready for the world without a sack full of books.

THEO: Some women have cosmetics. Eva has Kant.

GENE: Look who's talking! You're the one who insisted we buy a St. Christopher to stick on the dashboard.

THEO: Hey, he's the patron saint of travelers! Plus, it's not just a St. Christopher. This is the deluxe version with a bobble-head.

GENE: I do like how he nods approvingly when we come to a stop.

THEO: Finally! Here she comes.

Eva Lucien, only slightly larger than her overstuffed book bag, comes hurrying out of the library. On her way to the car, she runs into two disheveled characters and begins chatting with them.

THEO: Oh, you've got to be kidding me.

Theo honks. Eva waves goodbye to the questionable characters, rushes over to the Civic, and jumps in the back seat.

EVA: Sorry about that.

THEO: All right! California, here we come! First stop, Plymouth Rock!

GENE: Looks like you have plenty of reading.

EVA: I've got to cram. Grad school starts only three short months from now.

THEO: Already thinking about school! Eva! Vacation!

EVA: Grad school, Theo. I'm sooo far behind.

GENE: I think you can relax for a bit. By the way, who were those weir-does you were talking to?

EVA: Oh, that was my logic TA and a friend of his. They were having a really interesting conversation about consciousness, and…

THEO: Blah, blah. No philosophy, Eva!

EVA: Okay, okay.

GENE: I envy you, Eva.

EVA: Ah, is it my stunning good looks or my incomparable sense of humor?

THEO: Or her modesty?

GENE: No, really. I envy both of you. You're so sure about your next steps. You have a clear picture of your futures. Eva's going to grad school in philosophy, and you're going to seminary.

EVA: And you?

GENE: As far as I know, I'm going to spend the next year channel surfing in my parent's house in Atlanta.

THEO: What do you mean? You have the only degree that's actually use-ful! With engineering you can do anything you want. You can…

GENE: Yes?

THEO: Engineer things! With a philosophy degree Eva can flip burgers. And with English I can, what, compare the treatment of women in Henry Fielding and Henry James? Compared to us, you've got it made.

GENE: That would be great if I wanted to be an engineer. Or if I had any idea what I want to do. But I don't. None of my options look like the sort of thing I want to spend my life doing. You guys have a calling. You're driven. Meanwhile, I'm drifting.

EVA: Now *you're* the one who should relax. Graduation was a week ago. It's natural to feel a little untethered. That's why we're going to California!

THEO: Cali, baby! Woohoo!

GENE: You're probably right. But still, I can't shake the feeling that I should feel pulled by something—something to give my life some purpose, some meaning. Solving design problems just doesn't cut it.

THEO: Don't worry. Everyone has something they were put here to do. It'll come to you. The struggle is part of the journey.

EVA: Oh here we go. We weren't put here by anything. We were born because our parents got the itch, and we'll die when the oxygen stops. That's that.

THEO: That can't be all there is to it, Eva. What would be the point of it all?

EVA: I'm not sure I even understand that question. The point of taking a train is to get to where you're going. The point of telling a joke is to get a laugh. But is there a point to everything taken as a whole?

THEO: Of course! Otherwise, why do any of those things? I know this won't convince you, Eva, but that's one of the reasons why we know God exists.

EVA: There are so many problems with that reasoning, I don't even know where to start. You don't believe that nonsense, do you, Gene?

GENE: I have no idea what to believe about that. My family was kinda spiritual in their own way, I suppose. But my dad was Jewish and my mother was Methodist, so I was brought up confused. When I was five, I got a dreidel for Christmas.

THEO: What's a dreidel?

GENE: Never mind. Long story short, I just don't see how anyone can have any confidence one way or another in this area.

EVA: I do.

THEO: So do I.

GENE: Yeah, I don't get that. I know you're a believer, Theo. But what would you consider yourself, Eva? An atheist? An agnostic?

EVA: I'm a card-carrying atheist. No agnosticism for me. Too wishy-washy.

THEO: Even if you don't believe, I don't see how you can be an atheist. How can you be completely certain there's no God?

EVA: Well, there are no good arguments *for* God's existence, and there are good arguments *against* it.

GENE: Yeah, but surely you could be wrong! You've got to admit it's at least conceivable that when you die you'll find yourself in heaven.

THEO: If you're lucky.

EVA: You're overestimating what it takes to be an atheist. As an atheist, I believe God doesn't exist. I think I have good reasons for my view, but I don't have to say I'm 100% certain or that I couldn't imagine being wrong. I'm not sure we can be 100% certain about anything. I believe there are no unicorns or flying witches, but I can imagine waking up one day with a unicorn licking my forehead as a witch soars above on a broom. Don't you feel similarly, Theo?

THEO: I'm very confident in my belief. But sure, I suppose I can *imagine* I'm wrong. Barely, but okay.

EVA: Right. So, if you can believe in God without having absolute certainty, then you shouldn't hold atheists to a higher standard.

GENE: Okay, so let me get this straight. An atheist is someone who doesn't believe in God.

THEO: Right.

EVA: No, wrong. An atheist is someone who believes God doesn't exist.

GENE: What's the difference?

EVA: It's the difference between believing something is false and having no opinion on the matter. There are those who don't believe either that God exists or that God doesn't exist. Those guys are agnostic: they don't commit either way.

THEO: Look, if you don't believe, you don't believe.

EVA: No, there's a difference. For comparison, consider beliefs about the total number of stars in the universe. People in one group believe that number is even. People in a second group believe that number is not even, but they don't expressly say that the number is odd. Are they committed to a view on whether the number of stars is odd or even?

THEO: Yes.

EVA: Right! Their belief that the number isn't even logically commits them to believing that it's odd. So, they're not uncommitted. The truly uncommitted don't believe there's an even number of stars *and* also don't believe otherwise. These guys are like the agnostics: they think there's not enough evidence to believe either way.

GENE: Good. So it sounds like I'm an agnostic.

THEO: And I'm a theist, since I believe in God.

EVA: And I'm an atheist, and we're all in a Civic going to California. This sounds like a bad joke.

THEO: I'll tell you a bad joke: that guy's driving! He speeds up when I try to pass him and slows down when I'm behind him. There's a place in hell for people like that.

EVA: Maybe we'll be flame neighbors.

THEO: Don't joke about that. Seriously, though, if you don't believe in God, what's the point of life? Why not go around murdering people?

EVA: Hold on, now. There are two questions here. One's about morality, and another is about life's grand purpose—whatever that's supposed to mean.

GENE: Yeah, but I see a connection. I mean, they're both questions about what gives purpose to our actions. They both concern what we should and shouldn't do. The problem for atheists is that without God there's no basis for morality and no meaning to life.

EVA: Okay, maybe there's a connection. But I don't think God is necessary for morality. I think there's good reason not to murder—a reason that's independent of the God question.

GENE: Because if you go around murdering people you might get arrested and kept in a cell?

EVA: That's one reason, but it's not the only one. There's a reason not to murder even if you know you'll get off scot-free.

GENE: Which is…

EVA: Murder is wrong! If my main reason for not murdering you were fear of punishment, I'd be pretty immoral. And that's true whether I thought the punishment would come from the state or from God. I don't have to be threatened with jail or hellfire to respect someone's right to life.

THEO: Wait a minute, Eva. How can you call anything immoral if you don't believe in God? I don't think you can.

GENE: Sure she can. Without God, morality is a matter of social conventions; it just depends on what society approves of.

THEO: But then morality might vary from culture to culture. But that's implausible. If a culture suddenly decided murder was okay, would it be? If a culture decided to enslave blacks or kill Jews, would those practices be morally acceptable? I don't think so.

GENE: Huh. That does seem implausible. Well, Eva, are you willing to bite that bullet?

EVA: No, I'm not. I appreciate the help, Gene, but I don't buy that social conventions determine what's right and wrong either. I think morality is fundamentally objective.

GENE: Okay, then I'm with Theo; I don't see how you get that without God.

THEO: Yeah, and that's why I think there's an argument here for the existence of God. Have you ever read any Dostoevsky?

EVA: A bit. Why?

THEO: I think the argument I have in mind is implicit in several of his books. Take *Crime and Punishment*. You have Raskolnikov who doesn't believe in God and so feels unconstrained by conventional morality, believing he's above it all. So, he murders—and suffers underneath the guilt for the rest of the book. In the end, he embraces God. He realizes that you can't live life without a moral foundation and that there can be no moral foundation without God.

EVA: Yeah, that's a favorite Dostoevsky plot. Nabokov said Dostoevsky's characters had a habit of "sinning their way to Jesus." Nabokov didn't think that path was especially compelling. I agree.

THEO: Look, I'm not endorsing murder as a means to get in touch with God. But the underlying argument seems sound.

Eva: Again, what argument? Let's see a proof, a little one, two, three. You were a philosophy minor. Give it a shot.

Theo: Okay. Try this:

1. Morality—right and wrong—is objective and not just a matter of social conventions.

2. Morality is not objective unless God exists.

3. Therefore, God exists.

Gene: That sounds pretty good.

Eva: Well, I'll say this much for the argument: it probably lies behind the theism of many people—as well as the disdain in which many theists hold atheists. It's a loser, though.

Gene: Obviously you agree with the first premise, Eva, so you'll go after the second one. But what's wrong with premise 2? How can right and wrong be objective without God?

Eva: Well, the problem is—oh my God!

Theo: Do I hear a conversion?

Eva: No, did you see the guy in that car?! I think he was driving naked!

Gene: Probably an atheist. Okay, Eva, let's hear what's wrong with premise 2.

Eva: Okay. The point goes back to the *Euthyphro*.

Gene: The youth-fro? What's that, a children's hairstyle?

Eva: Har har. No, it's a one of Plato's dialogues. Socrates tries to get Euthyphro to define piety. For our purposes, though, we can think of Socrates asking for a definition of goodness.

Theo: Does Euthyphro give him one?

Eva: He tries. After some false starts, he says that good things are the things loved by the gods. Think of it like this: actions are good if and only if God commands them.

Theo: That sounds right.

Eva: Okay, but then Socrates asks the key question: "Are good actions good because God commands them, or does God command them because they're good?"

Gene: I think I get the distinction, but let's see. Is the question about what explains what? In other words, is God's reason for commanding certain things that those things are good? Or is it rather that His commanding them makes them good?

Eva: Precisely.

Theo: The answer is obvious. God is all-powerful. He's the cause of everything. So things are good because God commands them.

Eva: That's what I thought you'd say. But that answer can't be right.

Theo: Of course you think that. You don't believe in God.

Eva: No, that's not why. Even theists should believe that God commands things because they're good and not the other way around.

Theo: Why?

Eva: For one thing, if God suddenly said it's good to kill babies then, on your view, it *would* be good to do that.

Theo: Well, it might be hard to imagine, but maybe sometimes it *is* good to kill babies. God just knows more than we do.

Gene: You mean, for example, if we don't kill certain babies, they'll spread a disease that will quickly kill them and the rest of humanity?

Theo: Yeah, something like that. God wouldn't command it if He didn't have a good reason to.

Eva: That wouldn't be a case where something is good because God says it is. Killing the kids is good only because everyone will die if we don't kill them. That's not the kind of case I had in mind.

Theo: What sort of case were you thinking of, then?

Eva: Consider torturing babies for fun.

Theo: Do I have to?

Eva: Well, on your view it would be good to torture babies for fun if God commanded it. On my view, torturing babies for fun is bad, no matter what God commands.

Theo: But God would never command such a thing!

Eva: Why not?

Theo: Because God is good!

Gene: Uh-oh, Theo. I'm not sure that's a good response.

Theo: Why not? It's true: God is good!

Eva: Okay, then tell me this. Why wouldn't God command us to torture babies for fun?

GENE: What depraved creature could find torturing babies fun?

EVA: Look, just suppose some people derive pleasure from doing such despicable things. Given that supposition, why wouldn't God say, "Thou shalt torture babies—and thou shalt enjoy it!"

THEO: Because He's good. He commands only good things.

GENE: Yeah, Theo, but if things are good because He commands them, then His commanding us to torture babies would not be a case of His commanding a bad thing. Since He commanded it, it would be a good thing. It would only be a case of His commanding a bad thing if torturing babies for fun were independently bad.

EVA: Right. Put another way, what makes God good? If it's only because He says He is, then there's nothing contradictory about him commanding us to torture babies while at the same time proclaiming Himself good for making that command. If it's something independent about him—if His commands are good because they line up perfectly with the correct moral code—then things aren't good *in virtue of* His commanding them. Rather, His commands are good because they direct us to do good things—things that are good for independent reasons.

THEO: I don't follow you. You ask, what makes God good? The question makes no sense. God is good by definition. And what it means to be good is to be what God desires or favors.

EVA: You still have the same problem. On your view, there's nothing to stop God from commanding anything he wants to. And you're committing yourself to saying that if He commanded us to torture babies for fun, doing so would be morally good.

THEO: Okay, maybe I'll just bite that bullet: if God *had* commanded that, then that would have been good. The important thing is that He did *not* make that command. In fact, His commands entail that torture is bad, not good. So where's the problem?

GENE: Maybe it's just me, but I think torturing babies for fun would be bad no matter who or what commanded otherwise.

THEO: I can see that. But maybe you have that belief because God wanted you to. Maybe he made you such that you independently believe that the things He commands are true no matter what.

EVA: That move seems pretty desperate, Theo. Anyway, there's another, related problem here. Your view, that things are good because God commands them, seems to make God's commands capricious.

THEO: Why is that?

EVA: Well, imagine God trying to decide what to command. Suppose He asks himself: should I say, "Thou *shalt* covet thy neighbor's wife" or "Thou shalt *not* covet thy neighbor's wife?" On what basis would He decide which to command?

GENE: Ah, I see. He can't decide on the basis of which is good, because neither one is good yet, or rather, either one would be good if He commanded it.

EVA: Right. Then His decision would be based on pure whim. He might as well flip a cosmic coin.

THEO: Not so fast. It's true, God can choose whatever He prefers. But since He's good, what He prefers is guaranteed to be good. So, it's not whimsical after all.

GENE: I have a feeling of *déjà vu*.

THEO: What do you mean?

GENE: We're back to square one! What makes God good?

THEO: I've already answered that: He's good by definition.

EVA: I don't think that's going to help you. Let me make a comparison. Let's say that I'm by definition *evaish*.

THEO: What does that mean?

EVA: It just means doing things as I would do or would prefer to be done. So, now suppose someone says I'm constrained to command or do certain things by my evaish nature. There's a trivial sense in which that's true, but I'll be evaish no matter what I do. What is or isn't evaish will simply depend upon whatever whim seizes me at the moment. See the point?

GENE: Right! If God is good by definition in the same way, then He can't help but be good—not because He can't help but do or command the things we know to be good, but because whatever He does is called good.

EVA: Exactly.

GENE: That puts a new slant on all the church signs saying God is good.

EVA: Right, and that's why people who worship God should think that He commands things because those things are good and not the other way around. If God is good by definition, then saying, "God is good" is saying no more than "God is godish." It's no more a compliment to him than it would be a compliment to me to say, "Eva is so evaish." I can't help but be evaish! Vomiting on my shoes would be evaish if I did it. Saying God is good is only a compliment, or a reason to worship him, if goodness is valuable independently of whether God commands it. He's praiseworthy because He epitomizes this independent value, not because he's good by definition in the way I'm evaish by definition.

THEO: I think I see what you're saying. But isn't there a problem here? If God created everything, then He had to create all the good in the world, right? If there's something He can't make good—even something as awful as torturing babies—doesn't that mean He's not all-powerful?

EVA: I don't think this compromises God's power in any important respect. Think about triangles. Triangles have three sides, no matter what. That's just a necessary, unchanging truth. Even God can't make a triangle with four sides. It simply wouldn't be a triangle any more. That doesn't mean He didn't make every triangle in the world. He did, simply by making a bunch of three-sided polygons.

GENE: But doesn't that mean He's not literally all-powerful?

EVA: That depends on what you mean by "all-powerful." You could mean He's able to do anything that's possible. In that case, He could be all powerful despite being unable to make four-sided triangles or to make torturing babies for fun virtuous. Or you could mean He can do anything, period—whether it's possible or impossible. But is that even coherent? I don't think so. That makes omnipotence paradoxical.

THEO: Yeah, like that old chestnut, "Can God make a rock too heavy for him to lift?" People love to ask that.

EVA: Exactly. If you think God is all-powerful in the sense that He can do the impossible, then that question should trouble you. If He can make such a rock, then He's not all-powerful because there's something He can't lift. But if He can't make such a rock, then He's not all-powerful because there's something He can't create.

THEO: I hate that puzzle.

EVA: Some people love it and even try to solve it. If you ask me, though, the proper response is simple: just explain that when you say God is all powerful, you mean He can do anything *possible*. That's powerful enough, and it avoids the paradox.

THEO: So to bring us back to the discussion about morality, you would say His inability to make torturing babies for fun morally good doesn't imply that he's not all powerful—because doing that would be impossible, and an all-powerful being only needs to be able to do what's possible.

Eva: Exactly.

Theo: I like that. You may be convincing me about this. Maybe I should say that God says things are good because they're good, not that they're good because God says they are. Still, something makes me uneasy about this. Making goodness an independent constraint on God seems to compromise His perfection in some way.

Gene: Well, you can't have everything.

Theo: That's just it: God does have everything. I think I see a sort of compromise here. Maybe the problem comes from viewing goodness as separate from God's nature. Why shouldn't we say instead that goodness is part of His nature—part of what makes him perfect?

Gene: Interesting. But how does that view tie in to the Euthyphro question—are good things good because God says they are, or does God say they're good because they're good for independent reasons?

Theo: Here's the idea: God says they're good because they're good independently. Nevertheless, He's the source of goodness, because goodness is part of His divine nature.

Eva: So, let me make sure I follow you. On this view, goodness is objective. Not even God can make something good simply by deciding to call it good.

Theo: Yes.

Eva: But goodness still comes from God in the sense that it's part of His essence?

Theo: That's right.

Eva: Hmm. I'm not sure I quite understand what it means to say goodness is part of God's nature. But okay, I'll let that pass. Even if this compromise view makes sense, it doesn't save the initial argument.

Gene: Wait, I'm getting lost.

Eva: Okay, let's review. Theo gave a moral argument for the existence of God, which uses the premise that objective right and wrong depends on God's existence. I countered that even the theist should reject that premise. The theist should say that God's commands are good because they accurately represent and promote an independent value—because they correspond to a moral code that's correct independently of what

God commands. Otherwise, God's commands would be arbitrary and capricious.

THEO: Right, and I conceded that there's something to that counter-argument. But then I suggested a compromise view, which maintains the objectivity of morality but rejects the idea that morality is independent of God. I said that objective goodness is part of God's nature. On this view, God's commands aren't arbitrary, but moral value still originates from God. Problem solved.

GENE: Okay, I'm with you. But you can't stop there, Theo.

THEO: What do you mean?

GENE: Well, your view is consistent with the premise that objective morality depends on God; that much is true. But that's not enough. To make the moral argument work, you've got to establish the truth of that premise.

THEO: I realize I haven't defended the compromise view.

GENE: Yes, but that's not the only problem. The view is that objective morality is an essential part of God. That implies that if God exists, then morality is objective. But the moral argument requires the reverse claim-that if morality is objective, then God exists. Your so-called compromise view doesn't begin to show that.

EVA: Right. For comparison, take the view that my brain is an essential part of me. On that view, I can't exist without my brain. But the view does nothing to support the reverse claim—that my brain can't exist without me.

THEO: Okay, fair enough. Anyway, there's a variation of the moral argument that might be easier to defend.

GENE: Do tell.

THEO: It's simple, really: without God's commands, how would we know what's good and bad? How would we recognize which actions are right and which are wrong?

EVA: Those are interesting questions. What answer you give depends on what moral theory you subscribe to. And there are general issues about knowledge here too. That opens up a can of worms...

THEO: No worms in the car, please!

EVA: They're pretty interesting worms, but okay. I will say this, though. Goodness and badness have a lot to do with pleasure and pain. I don't think you need a divine revelation to realize that pain is bad and that pleasure is good.

GENE: True. A migraine would probably do the trick.

EVA: And think about this. You know those cartoons with Bugs Bunny or someone facing a moral choice? A little angel is on one shoulder advising him to do the morally right thing, while a little devil on his other shoulder cajoles him to do the opposite.

THEO: Yeah, I love those.

EVA: Me too. I've always thought there was a good idea for earrings there. So, the devil is always wearing red, holding a pitchfork and speaking in a gruff voice, while the angel is in white with wings, a harp and a plaintive voice.

THEO: As it should be.

EVA: But if there really were angels and devils like that, the devils would probably disguise themselves, speaking in sweet voices and wearing halos.

THEO: True. They'd have to be pretty dim-witted devils otherwise.

EVA: Right. So, suppose then you had a council on each shoulder. How would you know which was the angel and which was the devil?

THEO: That depends.

EVA: On what?

THEO: In part it would depend on what they said. Suppose one said, "Drive the car into oncoming traffic," and the other said, "No, don't do it! You'll kill yourself and your friends." Then I'd conclude the first one was the devil.

EVA: Right. You'd determine which was which by whether or not the advice given was, in your independent estimation, morally good advice.

GENE: Sounds right.

EVA: So in this case, you don't rely on what God says to determine what's good. On the contrary, you rely on your sense of goodness to determine which angel is God's messenger. So, you must be assuming you have independent access to what is and isn't good, absent God's word.

GENE: Alright, you've won me over, Eva.

EVA: You're an atheist?

GENE: Oh, no, not at all. I'm still an agnostic. I just agree that these moral arguments for the existence of God are unpersuasive.

THEO: I'm not completely convinced, but I do think there are better arguments out there.

EVA: There certainly are.

THEO: But I don't see how this helps with Gene's initial question: what's the point of all this? Can the universe have meaning without a God?

EVA: Actually, I'm suspicious about Gene's question. I'm not sure a universe is the type of thing that can have or lack meaning. Also, even if the universe can have meaning, adding God doesn't automatically give it one. Suppose God exists. Can't we ask the same question about that whole system, including God and heaven? Does *that* have any meaning? That question seems no less legitimate than Gene's. I can imagine an angel in heaven asking what the point of heaven is.

GENE: Wait—are you saying that I might still be obsessed with this question after I die? Am I that angel?

EVA: I certainly hope not. Anyway, if the answer to the angel's question involves pleasure, or love, or moral value, then that can be had on Earth.

THEO: Perhaps it can, to some extent. So what?

EVA: So the meaning-of-life question doesn't require a religious answer. Once we have a notion of objective right and wrong, our actions have a purpose: to promote the good and to prevent the bad. I'm not sure there's a further question.

GENE: Well, there's at least the further question about what makes you happy.

EVA: Yeah, but speaking for myself, I don't see why personal happiness has to depend on God. It's not as though ice cream becomes less sweet or a parent's love for her child becomes any less valuable if there doesn't happen to be an all-powerful being. Think of it this way. What's the point of our driving to California?

GENE: I hear San Francisco is heavenly.

EVA: Sure, but suppose we get there, and it's not so hot. Would all of this be in vain?

THEO: No, I think it'd still be worth the trip.

Eva: Precisely.

Theo: Speaking of the trip, there's the Plymouth exit! Get ready for stop number one!

Gene: I hear the rock is pretty disappointing.

Eva: Haven't we been over this already? Get excited, you jerk!

Gene: I hope they have T-shirts!

Theo: Hopeless. Completely hopeless.

2
Niagara, New York

Design and Evolution

Eva, Theo, and Gene are standing at the railing watching the water pour over Niagara Falls. Spray fills the air, and the friends have to yell to be heard over the roar of the waters.

THEO: Niagara Falls! See, Gene, wasn't this worth the trip?

GENE: It's a hell of a lot better than Plymouth Rock.

EVA: Yeah, that was a disappointment.

THEO: Well, what did you expect? It's a rock! Says so right there on its name. If it were called "Plymouth Laser Fandango," I could see disappointment. But as it is...

GENE: I don't know, I think I just built it up.

EVA: But even you have to admit, Gene, this is pretty awe-inspiring.

GENE: You're right; it's pretty damn cool.

THEO: Cool? It's things like this that make me believe in God.

EVA: What?

THEO: C'mon, Eva, you can't tell me you aren't impressed by the grandeur of it all. Even the most impressive of man's creations pales in comparison to the magnificence of these falls.

GENE: I'm not sure I agree with that. Have you ever used an iPhone?

THEO: Oh, give me a break.

EVA: You really think there's an argument from the existence of Niagara Falls to the existence of God? I mean, it says right here in the pamphlet how the falls probably arose, and God isn't mentioned.

THEO: The falls is just one example. The general idea is that nature contains amazing things, which must have been designed by God.

GENE: Unlike Plymouth Rock.

THEO: Right, unlike the rock. But really, we needn't have come to Niagara to discover something that demands explanation in terms of a creator who designed everything. We've been carrying examples with us all along.

GENE: You're not going to tell me you think God designed iPhones, are you? Please tell me you aren't.

EVA: No, I think I know what he has in mind.

THEO: I'll bet you do, Eva. So should you, Gene. This was in our Intro to Philosophy class freshman year.

GENE: I don't remember a whole lot from that class. I just remember being annoyed by some loudmouthed girl.

THEO: Oh, her. She was annoying. Always the first with her hand up, if she even bothered to raise her hand.

EVA: Correct me if I'm wrong, Theo, but I seem to recall you gradually moving seats until you were sitting next to me. And Gene, you weren't far behind.

GENE: I couldn't see the board! I had to move to the front row.

EVA: Uh-huh. And your excuse, Theo?

THEO: What can I say? You were the only girl in the class. Besides, we know how that turned out.

EVA: Don't remind me.

GENE: Okay, enough nostalgia, do you mind? Let's get back to what Theo was saying. What product of a great designer have we been carrying with us, Theo?

THEO: Our eyes!

GENE: You mean my eyes, which can't see the board unless I sit in the front row?

THEO: Yes, those. Weak as they may be, they're still miracles.

GENE: Thank you.

THEO: Remember Paley?

EVA: I do. In fact, I think I've got an article of his in my book bag.

GENE: Why didn't you leave that old thing in the car? It looks like it's killing you.

EVA: It's coming in handy, isn't it? I checked out a philosophy of religion anthology in the library, and lo! We need it here at Niagara Falls!

GENE: I'm not sure about needing it...

EVA: Here it is. Listen to this.

> In crossing a heath, suppose I pitched my foot against a *stone* and were asked how the stone came to be there, I might possibly answer that for anything I knew to the contrary it had lain there forever; nor would it, perhaps, be very easy to show the absurdity of this answer. But suppose I had found a *watch* upon the ground, and it should be inquired how the watch happened to be in that place, I should hardly think of the answer which I had before given, that for anything I knew the watch might have always been there. Yet why should not this answer serve for the watch as well as for the stone? Why is it not as admissible in the second case as in the first? For this reason, and for no other, namely, that when we come to inspect the watch, we perceive—what we could not discover in the stone—that its several parts are framed and put together for a purpose, e.g., that they are so formed and adjusted as to produce motion, and that motion so regulated as to point out the hour of the day; that if the different parts had been differently shaped from what they are, of a different size from what they are, or placed after any other manner or in any other order than that in which they are placed, either no motion at all would have been carried on in the machine, or none which would have answered the use that is now served by it. ...the inference we think is inevitable, that the watch must have had a maker-that there must have existed, at some time and at some place or other, an artificer or artificers who formed it for the purpose which we find it actually to answer, who comprehended its construction and designed its use.

> ...Every observation which was made ... concerning the watch may be repeated with strict propriety concerning the eye, concerning animals, concerning plants, concerning, indeed, all the organized parts of the works of nature. (Paley)

THEO: That just about sums it up. An old statement of the argument, but a good one.

EVA: It does sound compelling, I admit.

THEO: Actually, Paley's argument has problems.

EVA: Hey, I thought you were just endorsing it. Did I miss something?

THEO: I think a good argument can be made here. It just takes a little work.

EVA: I doubt that. Anyway, even if Paley's argument has problems, we should start by setting it out more explicitly.

GENE: We're at Niagara Falls. You can't possibly want to do philosophy now. I can't even hear half of what you're saying over the roar of the water!

EVA: We're at the Falls; we've seen the Falls. What do you think's gonna happen next? More water falling? I can forego the suspense. Let's go over to that picnic table.

Theo and Gene shrug and follow Eva.

EVA: Okay. Theo, does this capture the main steps of Paley's argument?

1. There are wonders of nature: natural things, such as the eye, with parts that function well together for a clear purpose.
2. The best explanation of the wonders of nature is that God designed them.
3. If that is the best explanation, then God exists.
4. Therefore, God exists.

GENE: What's all this about best explanation? I thought Paley was drawing an analogy between the watch and the eye.

EVA: Yeah, his argument is sometimes called "the argument from analogy." But the idea is, like the watch, the best explanation for the eye is that it was designed.

THEO: That sounds good to me.

EVA: Well, let's see. I think premise 1 is okay. I'm not going to deny that there are natural things that cry out for explanation.

THEO: There definitely are.

EVA: I'll also give you premise 3.

GENE: Wait. An explanation could be the best one we have and still be wrong.

EVA: That's true, but I wouldn't want to reject the argument for that reason. We're not looking for absolute certainty, after all. If Paley can show that the best explanation for a real phenomenon implies God exists, I'd concede to Theo.

GENE: What about premise 2, then? What's behind that one?

THEO: Isn't it obvious? How else could the eye have come about, if God didn't create it? It seems incredibly unlikely that it could have come about by chance. That's Paley's point. You might think a rock or a heap of sand came about by chance, but not a watch, and certainly not an eye!

GENE: Why not? Stranger things have happened.

THEO: Have they?

GENE: It's not impossible.

THEO: No one's saying it is. The point is that it's improbable.

GENE: Okay, but why? What's the relevant difference between a heap of sand and an eye? Why couldn't both have come to be by random chance?

THEO: Because heaps of sand aren't wonders of nature.

GENE: They might be to a sand lover.

EVA: Or a heap lover!

THEO: You're both missing the point. "Wonders of nature" is just an expression. The point is that the eye has a certain obvious internal complexity and coherence; its parts are put together just so, to make visual perception possible. The way the parts of the sand heap—the grains—are arranged is nothing like that.

EVA: True.

GENE: Well, even if I grant that it's unlikely that the wonders of nature arose just by chance, this doesn't prove there's a Judeo-Christian God of the sort described in the Bible. It doesn't even prove that God is still around! He might have designed the world and then taken a powder.

THEO: I admit that, but there are other reasons to believe the designer is the Judeo-Christian God. But we should proceed one step at a time. Showing that there was once a divine designer seems sufficient for step one.

EVA: If this argument proves that much, you're right. It would be one of the most powerful arguments in history.

THEO: It may well be, at least when properly formulated.

EVA: Hold on. We're not done assessing Paley's version. Back to your support for premise 2…

THEO: I just said it: it's much more likely that the eye was designed than that it came about by chance.

GENE: So you're saying that if something wasn't designed by a designer, it came about simply by chance. Why do you think that?

EVA: I agree that needs to be questioned, Gene. But before we even get to that, I wonder if positing a designer of the eye really does explain it any more than chance does.

GENE: Well, that much seems obvious to me.

THEO: Of course it's obvious. That's the point of the watch analogy. Surely if you were to stumble on a watch, you'd find the hypothesis that it was designed more plausible than the hypothesis that it resulted from some cosmic accident.

EVA: True, but that's because I understand how things like watches are designed and constructed. I don't have anything like that in the case of the eye.

THEO: But Paley's point is that we didn't make the eye: God did!

EVA: Yeah, but *how* did He do it?

THEO: Well, you can't expect to understand that. God's ways are beyond human comprehension. Yes, even yours, Eva.

EVA: That's just the problem. To me, a hypothesis that posits a mysterious, supernatural process—one we can't understand—provides no explanation at all.

THEO: I don't see why you think everything has to be intelligible to humans.

EVA: I don't think that. You're the one who's appealing to human intelligibility.

THEO: Let me make sure I understand the form of argument you're using. Is it, "I know you are, but what am I?"

EVA: Look, you say that the existence of the eye can be made more intelligible by assuming God made it, right?

THEO: Yes.

EVA: And do you mean "intelligible to God?"

THEO: No, to us.

EVA: Well there you go. You can hardly say that and then back off, claiming that God's ways are *not* intelligible to us. That would undermine the very reasoning you're using to establish God's existence.

GENE: Good point. But I have a different problem with Paley's argument.

THEO: What's this, Gang Up on the Theist Day?

GENE: No, no. Actually I'm pretty sympathetic to an argument like this. I mean, it makes God a fellow engineer. That's pretty flattering.

EVA: I thought you didn't want to be an engineer.

GENE: I go back and forth. But back to the argument: Theo, you seem to be presupposing that if the eye weren't created by an intelligent designer then it would have to have resulted from chance. Why do you think that?

THEO: How else could it have come about if left to nature? A bunch of molecules bang around and then suddenly, poof, an eye!

GENE: Um, have you ever heard of a little thing called evolution?

THEO: Oh, please. The theory of evolution is all about chance.

GENE: That's not true, Theo. Chance does play a role in natural selection, which is considered the main evolutionary mechanism. There's randomness to genetic mutations. But that's only one part of the story. It's not at all random that certain mutations become predominant in a population.

EVA: Gene's right, Theo. Natural selection explains a lot of what needs to be explained. It explains why parts of organisms are well adapted to their environment and why they function as they do.

THEO: How is that?

GENE: Well, mutations occur all the time. Most are complete flops, but every once in a while one confers a survival advantage on an organism. For example, maybe a mutation results in an organism's having a trait that helps it get to food a little more quickly or digest food more efficiently.

THEO: Are you suggesting it suddenly gets an extra muscle in its legs or an extra stomach?

GENE: No, the process is usually more gradual. Suppose some species of rodent lives in a desert. Because of a random mutation, one member of that species has fur that's a bit more like the color of the desert sand than usual. That small difference turns out to make it easier to hide from the local predators. Some of this particular animal's offspring have sandy-looking fur; fur color is a heritable trait. Those offspring therefore have a higher chance of surviving than the offspring of rodents with less sandy-looking fur color. The process repeats over and over. Eventually, the sandier fur color becomes a common or even universal trait in the population.

EVA: Right. And that creates an illusion of design. At any particularly advanced stage in the process, it can seem striking how well an organism's traits function. For example, you might compare the rodent's fur color to the sand and think, "Wow, what a good design. There must have been a designer!" When in fact there were many different so-called "designs"— many mutations that didn't confer any survival advantage and so didn't get passed on to later generations.

THEO: You know, it's fine to say that sort of thing in the science classroom and to propose it as a theory. But that's really all it is: a theory.

EVA: Aargh! You mean like the theory of gravity? That too is a theory, but I don't see you jumping over the falls. Scientific theories aren't just hunches!

THEO: Well, yeah, but the theory of gravity is testable. You can't confirm or disconfirm evolution in the same way.

GENE: That's not true, Theo. Also, now you aren't dismissing natural selection because it's just a theory. You're saying it's not a good theory.

EVA: Right. And remember, Theo. Your design argument bases the conclusion that God exists on the premise that His existence best explains the wonders of nature. So, you're advancing God's existence as a theory—a theory to account for observations of what we find in nature. There's no getting away from theories. The question is, which theory is better: design or natural selection? And I can't see how you can possibly maintain that the design theory is better. At least, I don't see many predictions, testing, and confirmation coming with the design theory.

THEO: Perhaps not, but evolution doesn't beat design on that score.

GENE: The theory of natural selection is actually well confirmed, Theo. It makes a lot of predictions, in that there's much we should expect to discover if it's true. And we have, in fact, made many of those discoveries.

THEO: Okay, give me an example.

GENE: Well, most obviously, it predicts that under the right conditions there'd be a fossil record that showed a general succession of species including some that aren't around anymore. It predicts that we'd find fossils far older than the biblical story of creation allows. Those have, of course, been found.

THEO: Okay, I see.

GENE: It predicts that there's a mechanism for the transmission of traits and that this mechanism would be susceptible to mutations. That was confirmed first by Mendelian genetics and then by the discovery that genes are composed of DNA. And once we knew about genes, evolutionary biology began making predictions Darwin was in no position to grasp.

THEO: Such as?

GENE: That complex organisms would have DNA in common with simpler organisms such as yeast, even if that DNA was no longer useful for those organisms. This has, in fact, been discovered.

THEO: Okay, but…

GENE: Hold on, there's much, much more. The theory predicts that species would be distributed in accordance with natural geographic boundaries. It predicts that where species span those boundaries there are explanations, perhaps in terms of continental drift. This has been found. It predicts that strains of bacteria would evolve to be resistant to antibiotics, forcing us to develop new ones. That has been confirmed. It predicts…

THEO: Okay, already, okay! I get the idea. There's a lot of evidence of that sort. I'd have to see the evidence myself to be fully confident in what you're saying.

GENE: I wouldn't have it any other way. You know, Theo, natural selection doesn't imply atheism. In fact, Darwin called himself an agnostic, like me. He wrote that the question of God's existence was too profound for the human intellect to answer.

EVA: Huh.

THEO: But look, aren't there things evolution predicts that we haven't found? For example, aren't there gaps in the fossil record? And aren't there aspects of life evolution can't explain?

GENE: There are gaps in the fossil record, but many of those we should expect. Soft parts, such as reproductive systems, aren't going to fossilize. With respect to others, just hang on. We haven't been searching very long in the grand scheme of things, and new fossils are being unearthed all the time.

EVA: I think Theo has other things in mind as well, though, Gene. Things that the theory of natural selection just doesn't explain.

GENE: Such as?

THEO: Well, Paley's eye example still seems to be a good one. I mean, not only is the eye a complex organ that plays a particular role, but it wouldn't confer any clear survival advantage for us if it were less than complete. That's a problem.

GENE: Why?

THEO: If the human eye came about all in one go, then sure, natural selection could explain why we all have eyes. But the eye was supposed to have developed gradually, in stages. And many of the earlier stages don't provide us with survival advantages. In particular, they don't help us see. So, the natural selection theory can't explain how the eye actually emerged.

GENE: Yeah, that's a famous example. Actually, Darwin thought of it himself.

THEO: And his answer was…

GENE: Part of his answer was that the early predecessors were not simply eyes without pupils or anything like that. They were probably nerves that were sensitive to light, and then the organ that played that role became better at it. Further mutations proved useful in that way and stuck for that reason. The organ's complexity therefore increased.

THEO: I can see how that might have happened. Why think it did in fact happen?

GENE: Well, organisms with primitive light sensors of the relevant kind have been found. So have organisms at what appear to be intermediate stages of evolution—creatures that would have enjoyed advantages over their predecessors.

EVA: I didn't know about that stuff, but it makes sense. Still, it seems Theo could come up with other examples, like the wing. It's hard to imagine the same story holding there—little wings probably don't help transport their bearers at all, certainly not through the air.

THEO: Look whose coming to my cause!

EVA: Remember, I jumped that ship a long time ago. I'm just trying to understand the details of the current theory.

GENE: It's a current theory in that the theory of natural selection evolves as new discoveries are made. Darwin couldn't anticipate certain features of trait transmission because he didn't know about chromosomes. Still, the basic structure of the theory remains the same.

THEO: Don't think you're getting out of explaining the wing, Gene. Let's hear it.

GENE: Well, evidence strongly suggests that fully functioning organs don't only evolve from more primitive devices that serve the same function. Darwin also pointed out that things playing one function can develop to a certain complexity and then, only at that point, begin to serve a completely different function.

THEO: And the wing...?

GENE: There's reason to believe that ancestral wings served to vent and cool creatures that had them. Those creatures couldn't fly, but their descendents could. Feathers have also switched roles in the same way. Some dinosaurs had feathers that helped enable them to fly, but in their ancestors, who couldn't fly, the feathers helped insulate them.

THEO: Okay, I guess that's reasonable. But surely you admit there are wonders of nature that don't have explanations in evolutionary terms. I've read something by a biochemist who says that some of the biggest problems for Darwin arise on the subcellular level.

GENE: What problems was he or she talking about?

THEO: The main one concerns the flagellum. What explains how some bacteria developed flagella as sources of motion? Apparently, flagella are astonishingly complex. A proto-flagellum—something that would have preceded the flagellum in evolutionary development—wouldn't have helped the bacterium survive.

GENE: Look, this game of cat and mouse seems silly. As science progresses and old puzzles dissipate, new puzzles emerge. That's not damning to evolutionary biology. On the contrary, it's exactly what we should expect if the theory is true. Advances are being made almost daily.

THEO: I don't know. The flagellum example seems to expose a weakness in the theory.

GENE: As a matter of fact, an evolutionary predecessor for the flagellum has been found, in the form of a syringe-like appendage that enables some bacteria to inject poison into their victims. It has most of the same proteins of the flagellum, but it's missing a few, and it performs a perfectly good function. The function is different from that of the flagellum, but it helps the bacterium survive all the same.

THEO: Huh. Maybe the example isn't perfect. But there are bound to be others.

GENE: Look, this is a common theme. An apparent counterexample to natural selection falls to scientific progress.

EVA: Yeah. Things tend to look particularly problematic for evolutionary biology only when its critics jump ahead and presuppose a particular developmental path for an advantageous feature—and then argue that natural selection can't explain that feature if it developed in that way. The wing case fits this pattern like a glove. Explaining the wing's emergence in terms of natural selection can seem hopeless if we assume the wing's predecessors would have to help creatures fly. But if we allow for the possibility of different developmental paths, involving changes in function, then natural selection can accommodate the example without much difficulty.

THEO: Okay, I admit I'm a bit out of my depth since I don't have the scientific facts on hand. But doesn't it seem to you that whatever story you tell is going to wind up being pretty incredible? Mind-boggling even?

EVA: Mind-boggling? You mean mind-boggling like an all-powerful spiritual being who created everything from nothing?

THEO: Given that God decided to create a world like this, it's beyond understanding but not surprising.

EVA: Remember, Theo, you're supposed to be *arguing* that God exists because He figures into the best explanation of what we observe. You can't just start off assuming God exists and then point out how easy it would be for Him to create what He wanted.

GENE: And I'd be interested in hearing more about what's so mind-boggling about evolutionary biology.

THEO: I heard an analogy once that thinking Darwinism explains the way things are is like imagining a tornado sweeping through a junkyard and accidentally assembling a working jet plane. It just seems absurdly improbable.

EVA: Theo! That analogy ignores everything we've been saying! Evolutionary biology does *not* maintain that the process is random!

THEO: Still, even given the theory you must admit that the way things are is really improbable.

GENE: Ah, I thought this might be a point about probability. You have to be very careful in drawing conclusions based on probability assessments. For one thing, just because an outcome is unlikely doesn't mean it's impossible. For example, suppose I deal you a hand of five cards. Let's say you have just a random assortment of cards, not falling into any order that's particularly valuable for poker or bridge or anything. Your getting that series of cards, especially in the order you received them, is very, very unlikely.

EVA: How unlikely?

GENE: 1 in 2,598,960 for getting five specific cards. For getting them in a specific order, it's much lower: 1 in 311,875,200.

Eva and Theo chuckle. Gene shrugs.

GENE: So, that's very unlikely. Still, it happened, and an equally unlikely outcome will happen if I deal you another hand.

THEO: Yeah, but if you deal me a royal flush, we have the intuition that this is especially unlikely and that you might have even rigged it. Why is that?

EVA: Wait! Gene, what are the chances of getting a royal flush, compared to getting any other poker hand?

GENE: That's really beside the point, Eva.

EVA: C'mon, you know you can't resist telling us.

GENE: Okay, okay: about 1 in 649,740. I'm not embarrassed that I'm good at math. But I want to answer Theo's question, about the intuition that if you're dealt a royal flush you might reasonably suspect foul play.

THEO: Good. Please do.

GENE: Let's say the royal flush is all spades. The important point here is that, as a purely random result, just getting those five particular cards is no less likely than getting any other five specific cards. But because we give it special status in advance of its being dealt, when it does come up we remark on how unlikely it is.

EVA: That's a good point. A similar point applies to life in general. Were we to stand outside of the universe at its origin and have in mind a future that included a particular set of organisms, it would seem incredibly unlikely that those things should arise. That's essentially what you're doing when you marvel at the fact that our evolution is so unlikely. But you start out looking for these preferred outcomes in part because you're among them and they include things you're familiar with. A purely impartial observer would see this particular outcome as you'd see a random deal of cards—as just one outcome among others.

THEO: You don't think this—the universe—is a preferred result?

EVA: Sure, I prefer it to some alternatives. But I'm hardly an impartial party to these proceedings!

THEO: No wonder you're so cynical.

GENE: There's another point about probabilities, Theo.

THEO: I'm still trying to get the last one. But go ahead.

GENE: It's important to remember that our estimation of probabilities in these cases is based on a background of ignorance. We don't know both the initial conditions and the way those conditions developed. If we knew more about these things, the outcomes might not seem so improbable.

THEO: I don't follow.

GENE: Take the case of the hand of cards. It's only improbable assuming it's completely random, but of course it isn't. Actually, given the particular way the cards were shuffled and the particular way I dealt them, that outcome was far from improbable: it was guaranteed! It only seems improbable because effective shuffling complicates things to the point where to our eyes no particular arrangement of cards seems likely.

THEO: Okay, so that's right in the case of the cards. But I don't see how it applies to the case at hand.

EVA: I do!

THEO: Of course you do. This conversation is doing wonders for my self-esteem. I might test the theory of gravity after all.

EVA: Here's an example. Suppose you knew nothing at all about biology, reproduction, or anything else. Then you find out your horse is pregnant.

THEO: My horse? Is that a euphemism? I own a Civic, not a Shetland pony.

EVA: Don't be difficult. Anyway, supposing you know absolutely zero about how horses reproduce, how likely would you say it would be that your horse would bear another horse?

THEO: Pretty likely.

EVA: No, remember, you're completely ignorant. First of all, you don't know how horses reproduce or that they reproduce only with horses.

GENE: And the occasionally ambitious donkey.

EVA: Right. You also don't know what happens inside the horse.

THEO: I guess I wouldn't know the likelihood, then.

EVA: Right. As far as you know, that horse might birth a dog, a chicken, a snake, or a pig!

GENE: Or William Shatner!

EVA: You might assess the odds by counting all the types of animals you know and then saying that the chances of its being a horse is one out of that number. I mean really, what are the chances it would be a horse? That would be like lightning striking twice in one place!

GENE: But then you learn a little about reproduction...

EVA: Right. And you discover the horse spent some special time with another horse...

GENE: And you realize that it's not improbable at all that the horse should bear a horse. It is, in fact, just about guaranteed.

EVA: A horse bears a horse, bears bear bears, but only buffalo buffalo buffalo.

GENE: Yes, and pretty much all spawn spawn spawn.

EVA: Ah, right. And in addition, of course, spawn spawn spawn spawn spawn.

GENE: True, just as horses bear horses borne by horses, but never mind.

THEO: You guys are truly weird.

GENE: In any case, you get my point about probability?

THEO: I think so. You're saying if we knew enough about the initial conditions of life on Earth and the rules for life's development, the fact that such complex organisms arose wouldn't seem particularly improbable.

GENE: Precisely. So, we shouldn't be too terribly impressed with probability arguments of the sort you mention.

EVA: Especially since the existence of God doesn't seem particularly probable, given that we haven't observed too many perfect all-powerful supernatural creatures. When we see a freshly trimmed lawn, we assume a lawnmower was involved as opposed to a lawn laser because we're familiar with lawn mowers. It's not that lawn lasers are impossible. It's just that they shouldn't be the first explanation we embrace, given what we've experienced. The same applies to the explanation of the existence of complex organisms. We should look to things we know, not to things we don't, to account for what we see.

THEO: Actually, I think I do know God exists.

GENE: Remember though, Theo, that's something you're trying to prove. You can't just assume it.

EVA: Anyway, it certainly doesn't look like the beings in this world have a perfect designer. If you look at the way particular organisms are actually put together, they sure don't seem to be intentionally designed by a perfect creator. Natural selection seems to fit much, much better.

THEO: How's that?

EVA: Stephen Jay Gould has a nice example: the riddle of the panda's thumb.

THEO: What about it? Don't tell me it evolved when pandas discovered hitchhiking.

EVA: No, but if we see a hitchhiking panda, I say we give it a lift. Actually, though, panda's don't really have thumbs.

GENE: Ah. That solves that riddle.

EVA: There's a little more to it. They do have an appendage that functions as a thumb. It's very important to their ability to thrive on the bamboo they love so well. The thing is, this appendage is really an enlarged wrist-bone recruited for a thumb's task.

THEO: So?

EVA: So, if you were to design a thumb for a panda, you'd design—well, a thumb! Not a single bone roped to a palm by muscles—muscles that were themselves remodeled to serve a new function, just as the panda's wrist-bone was.

THEO: How do you know what God would design?

EVA: I don't. But you're the one who argues that He must have designed the wonders of nature because they're put together so elegantly. The panda's thumb seems like something cobbled together from evolutionary necessity: jury-rigged from available parts, not built from the blueprint of an ingenious divine engineer. Biological history is full of such adaptations.

GENE: And what about vestigial organs and parts that outran their usefulness in previous stages of humans? The human tailbone, for example. Maybe the appendix and wisdom teeth as well. And so-called junk DNA.

EVA: What's that?

GENE: Portions of DNA for which no function has been identified. In some cases, we just haven't yet discovered the function. But in other cases, junk DNA may be an evolutionary artifact; it once had a function but doesn't any more.

THEO: Alright, alright. Darwinism can't be dismissed out of hand. It might explain what Paley was talking about.

EVA: Finally!

THEO: But I'm not giving up yet. Evolution isn't incompatible with the existence of God, after all.

EVA: True.

THEO: I mean, maybe evolution is part of God's excellent plan for the development of the world.

EVA: That's possible. But since we can explain what Paley noticed without positing a deity, there's no point in positing one. Or even if there is a point, there's no argument for it. That would be like saying dragons cause earthquakes and then saying, when confronted by the fact of plate tectonics, that dragons cause the plates to move. Use Occam's razor.

THEO: What's that?

EVA: It's a principle for choosing among competing theories. You can think of it as a rule: if you don't need to posit an entity in order to explain what needs explaining, then don't. So, for example, suppose we're trying to explain why planets travel in regular, nearly elliptical patterns around the sun. One explanation is the familiar one, based on gravity, mass, and so on. But there's also the gremlin theory.

GENE: The gremlin theory?

EVA: Invisible, incredibly strong gremlins swim around in space, pushing around the planets. These creatures happen to like ellipses.

GENE: That's silly.

EVA: Right, but why dismiss it? One reason is that it involves saying there are invisible space gremlins—a type of entity that we don't have any other reason to suppose exists. The familiar theory also involves saying something exists, namely, gravity. But we have plenty of reasons to believe gravity exists—reasons that extend far beyond the case at hand. By supposing gravity exists, we're not being uneconomical—we're not positing entities that we don't need to posit, in order to explain what we observe. By contrast, the gremlin theory *does* posit entities that we don't have to posit. In other words, one reason to reject the gremlin theory is that it violates Occam's razor.

GENE: I think Theo might have something more sophisticated in mind, actually.

THEO: Thanks, Gene, I do. There's something Darwinism can't explain.

GENE: Such as why Eva thought Paley was worth quoting?

THEO: No: how the conditions for evolution arose at all.

EVA: The conditions for evolution? Wait, evolutionary biology doesn't *try* to explain that, just like chemistry doesn't try to explain the structure of the atom.

THEO: But conditions require explanation nonetheless. In order for Darwin's wonderful process to even get started, there have got to be living creatures. Life must exist. And there have to be laws of nature. What explains all of that?

EVA: What, are you saying it's God's handiwork?

THEO: Well, why not?

EVA: Ah, that argument. Well, let's set that out...

GENE: Eva?

EVA: Yes, Gene?

GENE: Are you feeling a little chilly?

EVA: Now that you mention it...

GENE: We're completely wet!

EVA: My book bag!

THEO: Wild how over time a little bit of spray can have such a huge effect.

GENE: I know. What are the chances? It's mind-boggling!

EVA: To the car! To the hotel! I've got to dry out these books! The librarians will kill me!

GENE: Well, so much for Niagara Falls.

THEO: I think they're glorious. Divine. I don't care what you say.

3
From Niagara to Chicago

Life and Fine-Tuning

In the Civic, books are spread out across the dashboard, on the laps of Theo and Gene in the front seat, and all over the back, kept there in a subtle arrangement by Eva.

GENE: I think the books on the dash are dry, Eva. How are yours back there?

EVA: Still a little wet. Maybe we should rotate them so they can all get a little sun.

THEO: Just don't put any in front of me. I almost ran off the road when *The Complete William James* fell onto my lap.

EVA: Maybe we should put a less prolix author up there.

THEO: No: nothing in front of me. Still, it was odd that the book flopped right open to James' discussion of religion. What are the chances of that?

EVA: Pretty good, I'd say. It looks like the spine was broken at *The Varieties of Religious Experience*.

GENE: In addition, Theo, you'd probably ascribe importance to any page it fell open to. We tend to find significance where we look for it.

EVA: Like seeing the face of the man in the moon.

THEO: I don't think it's anything like that. I mean, we were just having a discussion about God, and plop! James falls in my lap affirming the existence of God!

EVA: Fine, it's a miracle. But before we left Niagara weren't you about to present another design argument for the existence of God?

THEO: I was. It's similar to Paley's, but it escapes your counterarguments.

EVA: How's that?

THEO: At best, your counterarguments show that the appearance of design is inevitable given Darwinism.

EVA: I wouldn't put it quite like that. The main point is that evolutionary biology provides a naturalistic, God-free explanation of the wonders of nature—the very things Paley thought we can't explain without supposing God designed them.

THEO: Right, right. But some real mysteries remain. Evolutionary biology explains how living things replicate and evolve. It doesn't explain why there's life in the first place.

EVA: Well, I'll give this much: there must be building blocks of life that evolutionary biology doesn't explain. But then again, it doesn't try to.

THEO: Well there's your miracle! Life itself is remarkable. Its very existence cries out for explanation.

GENE: Yeah, that's something I've struggled with myself. People always act as though evolution is the last word on whether or not the world requires a designer. But there's reason to infer a designer's hand much earlier in the process.

THEO: Exactly.

EVA: Well, let's at least set this new design argument out clearly. It goes like this:

    1. Life exists.

    2. The best explanation of the existence of life is that God designed it.

    3. If that is the best explanation, then God exists.

    4. Therefore, God exists.

THEO: That's a simplified version of the argument, sure.

EVA: Well, there's a gaping hole in it.

Theo: Don't tell me you're so skeptical that you deny the existence of life!

Eva: No. I had the third premise in mind.

Theo: What's wrong with it?

Eva: Suppose the design explanation works for life. It doesn't follow that the designer's still around, that she's particularly good, or even that there's only one designer as opposed to a committee of them. Paley's argument had those problems too.

Theo: Yeah, we discussed that sort of problem. And what I said earlier is still true: showing that the wonders of nature were intentionally designed is an important first step in a bigger argument for God's existence.

Eva: Right, okay. In this case, though, I have another worry about premise 2. Couldn't life have always existed? I mean, what if basic life forms were among the universe's original constituents?

Theo: What if they were? That fact would still require explanation.

Eva: Would it? I'm not sure.

Gene: I might agree with Theo on that. But I think your abstract philosophical approach to this topic might be misleading you here anyway, Eva.

Eva: How's that?

Gene: Think about how scientists describe the origin of the universe.

Theo: You mean the Big Bang Theory?

Gene: Right. On that theory, it's pretty clear that the universe's earliest stages were incompatible with life.

Eva: Why?

Gene: For one thing, on the Big Bang Theory, matter was initially too densely compacted to include anything as complex as life.

Eva: Okay, fair enough. But I still find the argument pretty unconvincing. More so even than Paley's argument.

Gene: Why?

Eva: Think about Paley's watch analogy. He said a watch found in a heath would demand explanation in terms of a designer, while a rock found in the same place would not. It seems to me that the lowest forms of life resemble rocks more than they do watches.

GENE: Maybe from your perspective, Eva. But from a much smaller, microscopic perspective, life is pretty impressive. It's much more impressive than mere inert matter.

EVA: It still doesn't capture the imagination in the same way as the organs of plants and animals. But maybe you're right: that might just indicate something about my imagination.

THEO: Just think of a teeny weenie watch, Eva, on a very small heath. Along comes a very small … theologian, and…

EVA: Okay, Theo, spare me. I'll grant that the existence of life is impressive and seems to demand explanation.

THEO: Good. So, the atheist had better be able to plausibly explain the emergence of life.

EVA: I don't think a secular explanation for that is impossible.

THEO: No, you're making the challenge too easy. You not only need to show that it's *possible* for life to emerge from nonlife. You've got to show that life's emergence is *likely* without a helpful divine hand.

EVA: Now you're making the challenge too hard. For one thing, you don't get a proof that God exists just because I don't know enough to explain how life emerges. It could be that there's a way that I just don't know. In fact, I'm sure there is.

THEO: I'm not talking about just you. I don't expect you to know everything, although I'm surprised to hear you admit it.

EVA: Ha ha.

THEO: Anyway, if science can't find an explanation, that's a problem for atheism, isn't it?

EVA: Not unless you have an argument that science will never find an explanation.

GENE: Actually…

EVA: Also, even if we never figure out how life emerged naturally, that doesn't mean that it didn't.

GENE: Well, really…

EVA: And lastly, it's not right that atheists have to show that it's likely that life emerged naturally. It just has to be *more* likely than the alternative, involving an intelligent designer. So, you see…

GENE: Eva!

Eva: What?

Gene: Let someone else talk. Me, for instance.

Eva: Oh, sorry. I didn't know you had something to say.

Gene: I was going to say that in fact there's compelling evidence that life can emerge from nonliving components—and that scientists are getting closer to understanding how it probably did emerge on our planet.

Eva: Oh, good. See, Theo? Tell us all about it, Gene.

Gene: Well, a lot is unknown about the emergence of life, but serious progress has been made. As early as 1953, experiments showed that some of life's basic building blocks can emerge from stuff that was probably around relatively early in Earth's history.

Eva: Cool.

Gene: And new discoveries are made all the time. Some of those chemicals—the building blocks of life—have been found in meteorites. Scientists take that to indicate that such building blocks might be abundant in the universe.

Theo: Hold on. That last point doesn't help you. So the building blocks came by way of Meteoric Mail. What explains how they arose in the first place? Saying, "They came from outer space" just relocates the problem.

Gene: Yeah, that's true. And there are real puzzles here. It's not known how exactly proteins can arise from simpler components. That's something scientists are working on right now. But they're making progress. For example, it the past year or so, it was shown that some of the basic components of DNA and RNA can form as a result of spontaneous chemical reactions—reactions of the sort that might well have occurred early on in Earth's history.

Theo: Wait. So scientists have shown how life emerged?

Gene: No, as I said, there are unsolved problems. But scientists are optimistic that these problems will be solved, possibly in the near future.

Eva: The race is on for the Nobel Prize.

Gene: Probably more than one.

Eva: So, it looks as though it *is* reasonable to conclude that life arose naturally from nonlife. God's hand isn't needed here.

Theo: I'm not sure about that, Eva. Even if you're right about most aspects of life, how did *conscious* life emerge? Isn't that still a puzzle?

GENE: Why would conscious life be any more difficult to explain? Or are you just bringing up yet another thing that as a matter of fact hasn't been explained at this point?

THEO: No, I think there's something about consciousness that might be particularly challenging. Like, perhaps we can come to understand why people say "Ow!" when certain nerves fire, but can we really come to understand why there's something it feels like?

GENE: I still don't get it.

EVA: Actually, I'm a little sympathetic with Theo about this—at least about the claim that conscious experience might provide unique challenges for explaining the world in physical terms. As a matter of fact, Darwin's Bulldog, T.H. Huxley, thought this might be a particular problem. He said,

> How it is that anything so remarkable as a state of consciousness comes about as a result of irritating nervous tissue, is just as unaccountable as the appearance of the Djin, when Aladdin rubbed his lamp. (Huxley)

GENE: Just had that quote on hand, did you?

EVA: It's on my logic TA's webpage. He's kinda obsessed with the issue.

THEO: So the idea is that while the physical sciences might eventually explain things like life, reflex actions, or even basic thought, all of that could be done in terms of the very sophisticated movements of things in space. But no such explanation could possibly explain why we have certain sensations when smelling a cup of coffee.

GENE: This just sounds like the same old thing to me. We don't know how to explain it now, but I wouldn't bet against science. Lots of things seem really mysterious before great minds focus on the problem. Conceptual revolutions like the one caused by Einstein could be just around the corner.

THEO: I don't know, there seems to be something different here.

EVA: I agree, but the real issue is why this gives any sort of reason to believe in God.

THEO: Well, basically, natural science can't explain one of the most glorious phenomena in the universe, consciousness. And it needs an explanation, so the best explanation is supernatural: God.

EVA: Hold on there, Theo. Just because consciousness isn't explained by traditional physics doesn't mean that it's not natural. Conscious properties could just be another set of law-governed, natural properties. Maybe they just can't be explained completely by physics.

GENE: Yeah, but it's still puzzling that there would be these additional, miraculous basic properties, in addition to fundamental physical phenomena.

EVA: Well, perhaps, but it seems to be running in the wrong direction to explain the existence of these basic feeling properties in terms of a physically inexplicable, all-powerful creative spirit. That's like using a rocket launcher to kill a cockroach.

GENE: Those little buggers can be hard to kill.

THEO: Okay. I'll admit there's a jump from nonphysical to supernatural, and that God is a big gun to bring in here. But still ... it seems this sort of thing should lead to a little more modesty on the side of science.

GENE: Maybe, but I don't think so. Just as in the case of life, an explanation is probably forthcoming. It's just not clear to us at the moment.

THEO: Well, suppose you're right, Gene. Suppose even conscious life emerging naturally from physical components is possible. Still, if it's sufficiently unlikely that it did emerge in that way, an explanation involving a higher being might still be needed. Anything that's too unlikely is unacceptable as an explanation.

GENE: But why think life's emerging naturally is unlikely? Remember, we shouldn't let our ignorance about a process lead us to conclude that it's unlikely that the process occurred. There are different theories about how life originated on Earth, and none is generally accepted. Some scientists think numerous reactions had to occur involving elements that were both native to Earth and that were delivered to Earth by comets, meteorites, or space dust.

THEO: You've got to admit that sounds like a very improbable sequence of events.

GENE: I have heard people say that. One theorist I read about says that, based on the 1953 experiments, the chances of the components of life all coming together are one in 2.29 times 10 to the 105th power!

EVA: Wow. That's even less likely than your finding a girlfriend, Gene!

THEO: Now, now, Eva. You're forgetting about that girlfriend he had one summer in Canada.

EVA: Oh right, I forgot.

GENE: Okay, have your fun. Some of us are trying to have a real conversation here. There are several things worth mentioning about these supposedly low probabilities for the emergence of life.

EVA: Yeah, like how are those probabilities calculated?

GENE: One does wonder. I imagine it's by taking all the elements and calculating all their possibilities for combination, and then considering how many times the right combinations would have to happen for life to arise. Something like that.

EVA: But doesn't this run into the problem we ran into when talking about the likelihood of the development on the flagellum?

THEO: Wasn't that a point about evolution? We're talking about conditions that preceded evolution.

EVA: This is a point about assessing probabilities, not about evolution. You can't get an accurate probability assessment just by imagining a set of initial conditions and then assuming things happened randomly from there.

THEO: Why not? How else would you calculate it?

GENE: I think Eva's point is that we can't really know how likely it was that life should have arisen naturally, given how much we don't know about when and where it happened.

EVA: Right. All we can say is that if things happened randomly, and they happened in the hypothesized initial conditions, the emergence of life would be very improbable. Remember that to someone completely unfamiliar with biology, who knows nothing whatsoever about reproduction, it would seem no more likely that a pregnant horse would give birth to a horse and not a hamster.

THEO: Ah, right, the horse example.

EVA: To some extent, we're in a similar condition of ignorance when we speculate about the origins of life. We don't know enough about what the initial conditions were or how things proceeded from there to conclude that the emergence of life was wildly improbable.

THEO: I don't know, guys. It feels like I'm shooting at a moving target here. First you claim science can explain everything, and then you take refuge in our ignorance of the mysteries of the universe such as how life began.

GENE: Well, we shouldn't pretend to know what we don't! Science is an ongoing process. One way to put Eva's point about probabilities is that we shouldn't jump to conclusions until we have sufficient knowledge.

EVA: Exactly.

GENE: Nevertheless, I admit that when one thinks about all that has to happen for life to emerge on Earth, it can seem ridiculously improbable. But that leads me to another point. Even if the probabilities are very low, it's not clear that this should trouble us or lead us to prefer a divine solution.

THEO: Great, you don't even think your story needs to be probable to beat mine. How is that fair?

GENE: Well, I might admit it's not probable in a sense. It's almost certainly improbable for any particular planet that conditions would be right and life would arise.

THEO: That's what I'm saying.

GENE: But there are so many planets out there, that even improbable events are bound to happen sometime on some planet. I mean, think about this. Our galaxy, the Milky Way, has more suns and potential solar systems than there are grains of sand on all the beaches on Earth.

EVA: Wow. That's a nifty fact.

GENE: Yep. And our galaxy is just one of many—hundreds of billions. In fact, there are more galaxies than there are grains of sand on Earth.

EVA: So, there are a lot of chances in the universe for life to emerge.

GENE: A whole lot. So many that even if it's really unlikely that life would develop on any particular planet, it's a near certainty that life would develop on some planet or other.

THEO: Near certainty? That seems too strong. Lots of things have to be in place for life to develop. Things like the distance between the planet and the nearest star, the age and size of the planet, and so on. And even where the necessary conditions have been met, it may still be improbable that life will in fact develop.

GENE: If it's not a near certainty, it's at least not wildly improbable.

THEO: Okay, but even if that's right, isn't it extremely lucky that it's our planet that developed life? That Earth developed life?

GENE: I'd put it this way: we're precisely as lucky or unlucky as anyone who is in a position to ask that question.

EVA: What are you, a Zen monk? That's no kind of answer!

THEO: No, I get Gene's point. He's saying that people who are having this conversation are bound to be the so-called lucky ones. In other words, it's not like we were in a life lottery and we happened to win it. In this lottery there are no losers, because only the winners play!

GENE: Right. And there's one last point I wanted to make. It's about this low probability business. I'm not sure your position is totally coherent, Theo.

THEO: What do you mean?

GENE: Unless you just don't believe the science, it looks like this is, according to you, the path God chose to make life.

THEO: That's right.

GENE: Don't you see the tension in your argument?

THEO: No.

EVA: I do! I do!

THEO: I don't doubt it, Eva. But if there's a problem, I'd rather have Gene explain.

EVA: Why?

THEO: Because you're annoying me. Gene?

GENE: Well, it seems odd to insist both that the process by which life emerged, according to our best estimates, is convoluted, improbable, and inefficient, while at the same time saying that an all-powerful, intelligent being who wanted to create life chose this way to do it. I mean, one would expect that the process God would choose would be much more streamlined.

THEO: I'm not necessarily subscribing to the scientific story about how life emerged. That's your deal, not mine.

GENE: Oh, I thought your view was that science was getting it right—or would eventually get it right—but that God determined that it would go that way and stood by to make sure things went as planned.

THEO: I didn't say that, did I? I didn't mean to say that.

GENE: I thought you did, but anyway there's a dilemma here. If you agree with the scientists about the origins of life on Earth, then the process employed by your God inherits all the supposed awkwardness and inefficiency of the process science describes.

THEO: Okay.

GENE: And if you don't say that, and insist that God just planted basic life on Earth around four billion years ago, you have to bet that science won't eventually be able to give evidence for a nondivine origin. That's a risky bet. And you'd still have an odd story. If God is a life lover, why not make Earth hospitable to life earlier? Why not make more planets hospitable to life? The universe is a pretty empty and lonely place, all things considered. It doesn't look like the sort of place a life-loving god would create.

EVA: It looks, in fact, like a universe where life emerges only under certain select, somewhat improbable conditions of the sort that the scientists are beginning to describe.

GENE: Right.

THEO: Look, I see your point. But aren't you guys just placing your faith in science instead of God?

EVA: I know there's such a thing as science. I don't need to have faith. Don't you believe there's such a thing as science, Theo?

THEO: Funny. That's not what I mean by having faith in science. I mean you guys have faith that it will deliver all the answers. How is that better than faith in God?

GENE: Well, first of all, I'm not necessarily criticizing your faith…

EVA: I am!

GENE: …I'm just criticizing your arguments. More importantly, though, I don't actually believe that science will answer all of our questions. I think some questions might have to go unanswered.

EVA: I guess I'm more optimistic than Gene.

THEO: So you have blind faith in science.

EVA: I don't know that I'd call it *faith* in science, Theo. We have *evidence* of science's progress, and we can form expectations based on its past successes. That's not faith. It's reasonable belief.

THEO: Are you saying all faith is unreasonable?

Eva: Of course!

Gene: Whoa now, let's not go there. In this case I think you're both right. We do have reason to believe science will continue to succeed, but we shouldn't assume that it can explain everything.

Eva: Traitor!

Gene: I'm not saying I believe in God, or even that science will fail in its ambitions. I'm only saying that there are some things that need explaining and that science couldn't possibly explain.

Eva: How can you be so confident about that? You could just be another ignorant Paley.

Gene: My reasons are pretty simple, actually. Science explains things partly in terms of the laws of nature. There could be no scientific explanation without such laws. But at the end of the day, we ought to wonder why the natural laws are as they are. Something needs to explain them, and ultimately it can't be science.

Eva: Why not?

Gene: Because scientific explanations rely on laws. So, a scientific explanation of the laws would involve further laws. Those would themselves require explanation, and so we'd be back at square one.

Theo: That's pretty compelling. Explanation has to end somewhere.

Eva: Maybe. I'm not sure I still have a grip on what we're supposed to be explaining. If we're talking about laws of biology or chemistry, then sure, those require explanation. But what about fundamental laws, as in basic physics? Why think those laws need explanation? They just are what they are.

Theo: Yeah, but it's pretty lucky that they're precisely this way. They could be another way, a way that would never allow life to arise.

Gene: That's right. This is sometimes called the fine-tuning argument. The universe isn't simply a haphazard and chaotic assembly of matter and energy. Things are well ordered, and they seem to be particularly well tuned for life to arise. Most other "initial settings" for the universe wouldn't even allow planets to arise, much less life.

Eva: Why think the initial settings could have been different than they are, though?

Gene: Why think they couldn't? There seem to be many alternate possibilities. For example, immediately after the Big Bang, the universe could have collapsed back in on itself, or expanded far too quickly for galaxies to form. To avoid these problems, the early rate of expansion would have to be within 1 in 10 to the 55th of what it was. Another example: if the nuclear weak force had been much weaker or stronger, there could be no hydrogen in the universe—thus no water, among other things. The nuclear strong force needed to be about what it is, or there could be no protons. There are other examples involving the gravitational and electromagnetic forces, but you get the idea.

EVA: I get the idea but I'm not sure about how you're calculating probabilities here. Your point is that you can change the constants a bit—change the weak force, say—and get no life as a result. But that doesn't show that life is improbable. To determine whether life is improbable, you need to consider a bunch of scenarios with different constants, randomly assigned, and see what percentage leads to conditions consistent with life.

GENE: True. But won't that give us the same conclusion?

EVA: Actually, it's not so clear that it will. In fact, I read about a scientist who developed computer models to test these ideas. According to his calculations, about a quarter of the scenarios were consistent with life.

GENE: Huh. I'd like to see those calculations; that result is surprising.

EVA: I just wanted to raise the possibility that your assumption about the improbability of life is incorrect. But I don't think the argument works anyway, so I'm willing to grant your assumption for the sake of argument.

THEO: I think it's a very plausible assumption. It appears that we're very lucky that the universe is hospitable to us. Let's go back to Paley and use your tuning analogy. Imagine him walking along a heath and finding a radio with a huge dial.

EVA: Huge dial? What do you mean, a big knob?

THEO: No, I mean there are just tons and tons of frequencies the radio picks up. Anyway, the radio is tuned to the only live frequency in the universe. Had the tuning knob been turned even slightly one way or the other, there would be no music.

EVA: Okay.

THEO: So, what should he conclude?

EVA: That people keep throwing their junk in heaths?

THEO: He should conclude that someone turned the knob until the one station was found. To suppose it just randomly appeared set in that way would be ridiculous. In our case, of course, the tuning hand had to belong to a divine creator.

GENE: Speaking of which, let's see what's on the radio.

EVA: Hey, we're talking here.

RADIO: *Desperado...*

THEO: Oh man, it's the Eagles. Shut it off.

EVA: I hate the Eagles.

GENE: Alright, alright. I was hoping to find a little Creedence.

EVA: You were hoping to get out of the conversation.

GENE: That too.

EVA: Theo, I'm not sure your radio analogy is so hot, even if everything Gene says is right.

THEO: No?

EVA: No. The most important difference is that in the radio case our observations could have been different. Paley could have stumbled on the radio and found it tuned to a different station.

THEO: Same thing with the universe: its initial settings could have been different.

EVA: Yes, but if they had been different no one would have been around to observe that fact. In other words, any observer taking note of the settings of her universe would determine that it was fine-tuned—because poorly tuned universes don't have observers, by definition. Gene made this point earlier. Remember the Zen-master comment?

GENE: I see what you're saying, Eva, and it is like the argument I made earlier. But I don't see how it applies here.

EVA: I'm making a general point about using unbiased observations in estimating the likelihood of the truth of a hypothesis. Since the very fact of our making an observation guarantees that there's a finely tuned universe, we can't count that observation as part of our evidence for how likely it is that our universe is finely tuned.

THEO: I still don't get it.

EVA: Think about it this way. See that lake over there?

THEO: Oh, this is going to be good. Yeah, I see the lake.

EVA: Suppose you're using a net to fish in that lake and you pull out lots of fish, all of which are over six inches long. What can you conclude about the fish in that lake?

THEO: That they're all or mostly over six inches long?

EVA: That's what it might look like, but suppose you discover that your net is porous. It's so porous that any fish under six inches long would almost certainly escape. Now what should you conclude?

THEO: Well in that case you should conclude nothing about the average fish size.

EVA: Right. Your means of observation guarantees that you observe a biased sample. The same thing is true in the case of the universe. We're guaranteed to observe a finely tuned universe, so that observation should itself carry no weight with respect to the likelihood of a fine-tuned universe.

GENE: That's an interesting point, Eva, but I'm not sure I buy it.

EVA: Why not?

GENE: It seems to me that you're right about one thing: we shouldn't be surprised that we aren't observing a universe that isn't finely tuned.

EVA: Obviously.

THEO: Of course. I agree with that. We couldn't observe a universe that's not fine-tuned because by definition it wouldn't generate observers.

GENE: Right. But that doesn't show we shouldn't be surprised that our universe is finely tuned.

EVA: But why should you be surprised in one case and not the other?

GENE: Compare this case. Suppose you don't really like sports…

EVA: That's easy enough.

GENE: But suppose you do watch the news and so watch the occasional highlight reel from the previous week's football games.

EVA: I hate those things.

GENE: Still, suppose that when watching you see a truly amazing catch or something. You see a guy, let's say, flip over another player and catch the ball while doing his flip.

EVA: Okay.

GENE: Well, you shouldn't conclude that football is an amazing sport filled with moments like that, because you know you're watching a highlight reel. And you know highlight reels tend to show amazing plays.

EVA: That seems right.

THEO: And, tell me if I'm wrong, Gene. You shouldn't be surprised that you're not watching a boring moment in sports, since the highlight reel wouldn't show such moments.

GENE: Exactly. You shouldn't make either of those inferences. Either could result from selection bias, as in the fishing-net case. But that doesn't mean that you shouldn't be astonished that such a catch should happen. You might believe that you've just seen a superhuman athlete or that you've seen an incredibly lucky catch. Either way, you should think what you see requires explanation.

THEO: That sounds right. So the fact that the universe seems tuned is like the fact that the catch seems impressive. Both cry out for explanation.

EVA: Okay, I get your point, and it's a good one. But I think there's a flaw in your analogy.

GENE: Let's hear it.

EVA: In the case of football, even people like myself who don't know anything about the game know something about the human body as well as about gravity and other basic matters of physics. So I know that two-hundred-and-fifty pound men don't just toss in the wind like feathers. I also know, based upon my own sense of disorientation, that when I spin around too fast that it's hard to keep track of objects, much less catch them, in such circumstances. Add to this that I can't reliably catch a tennis ball if you toss it to me, and yeah, I'm pretty surprised to see your football player making a catch mid-flip.

THEO: So?

EVA: I don't have any such knowledge when it comes to universes as a whole. So while I can look at one football catch and be amazed that it happened, I don't have the same sort of background knowledge to look at a universe and be amazed that it happened. I also don't know enough about gods to be able to say that a fine-tuned universe is one they would particularly favor.

THEO: Those are decent points. Even so, I can't shake the sense that it's incredibly unlikely that such a hospitable universe appeared by chance, without the help of a divine hand.

GENE: I'm not sure what I think. While we were chatting, though, I was browsing through one of these books on the dashboard.

EVA: Is it dry?

GENE: It's a tad dry, but it's still interesting.

EVA: Very funny.

GENE: I couldn't resist. Anyway, as it happens, this book concerns ... the fine-tuning argument!

THEO: My God! What are the chances?

GENE: Yes, well, the author, John Leslie, agrees that the fine-tuned-ness of our universe requires explanation. His favored explanation, though, isn't that the universe was intentionally designed but that there are multiple universes.

THEO: What? That's crazy.

GENE: Not really. He points out that if there were many universes, each with slightly different initial settings and laws, it wouldn't be surprising that one of them was conducive to and eventually produced life.

EVA: How could there be multiple universes? You do mean universes, right, not galaxies or something?

GENE: Right: they have to be universes, because they have to be completely independent systems governed by distinct laws and distinct physical constants.

THEO: I agree with Eva. In fact, this is making my head spin. Let's stop for a while.

The car pulls into a rest stop, and the trio moves to a picnic table. Theo lies in the grass.

GENE: I wouldn't lie down around here, Theo.

THEO: I'm so tired I can hardly see.

GENE: Well then maybe you don't see all the people walking their dogs around here.

Theo jumps up and brushes himself off and sits at the table.

THEO: Okay, so tell me about these many universes of yours.

GENE: Well, by hypothesis they aren't detectable by scientific instruments or anything...

EVA: Theo won't hold that against you. He doesn't have a god-o-meter either.

GENE: There are several possibilities. One is that the universe expands and collapses in a cycle, with each explosive expansion governed by a separate set of laws.

EVA: Huh.

GENE: Another possibility is that there just happen to exist many separate systems that aren't causally connected to each other. Light doesn't travel from one system to another. If these systems exemplify different regularities, they could function as different universes.

THEO: Um...

EVA: Okay, I'm not sure I fully grasp these scenarios. But I'm not sure I need to. The idea of multiple universes doesn't sound any weirder than the idea of an intelligent being intentionally creating everything by some sort of supernatural magic.

GENE: The multiple universe view makes total sense to me. And if it's coherent, then it provides a partial answer to the fine-tuning argument. Even if the constants and laws of the universe require a special explanation, there's a nontheistic one available.

THEO: Wacko explanations are always available.

GENE: The multiuniverse story is strange, I'll admit. But it's actually better in some obvious ways than the God-made-it explanation. I mean, at least I know what a universe is and how to investigate its nature scientifically. I'm not similarly familiar with gods and their handiwork.

THEO: Speaking for myself, I have a better grip on God than I do on anything so abstract as a universe.

EVA: Neither one sounds particularly compelling to me. It seems to me that both of you are making an assumption, quite frankly.

GENE: Which is...

EVA: You're assuming life is such a special result that a special story is needed to explain how it's even possible. That's not obvious. The universe had to be some way, and any particular way it turned out to be would be equally dependent upon a particular arrangement of initial settings and conditions. Of course we think this particular outcome is nifty, because we find ourselves nifty. But maybe this is just a consequence of a false sense of self-importance. You see that couple over there necking at the other picnic table?

GENE: Yeah, I noticed. It looked like a little more than necking. Excessive public affection, I'd say.

THEO: Don't be a prude, Gene.

EVA: It looks like they're in love.

THEO AND GENE: Awww.

EVA: And like many people in love, they're probably convinced that they were made for each other. They believe they're meant to be together— soul-mates, brought together by the hands of destiny.

THEO: I'm not sure destiny's hands are the busy ones in this case.

EVA: Stop staring, Theo. My point is that they are, of course, wrong. They believe their love was destiny only because they're stunned by the sense that what they have together is so damned wonderful.

THEO: That's a tad cynical, Eva, even for you.

EVA: But you see what I mean, don't you? The subjective impression of something's importance can make it seem in particular need of explanation, even if from an objective standpoint that thing is no more important than anything else.

GENE: That's true. She probably won't think much explanation is needed when it turns out he's a selfish womanizer.

THEO: Cynics all around! I'm surrounded by them!

EVA: I may be cynical, but the fact remains: we should be reluctant to infer too much from our sense of our own splendidness.

GENE: So we see our existence as evidence of a divine design only because we build in a lot of assumptions about the desires, powers, and beliefs of the deity in question?

EVA: Exactly. A creator's intellect might be radically different from our own. To assume she would design things in this or that particular way, with this or that particular result in mind, seems reckless.

GENE: There's another problem with the fine-tuning argument for God. The fact that there's a universe that contains life at best only raises the probability of there being a divine creator. Nothing says it raises the probability to a particularly high level.

THEO: Surely if the reasoning is sound, it's at least *reasonable* to believe in God as creator.

GENE: Not necessarily. That depends upon how likely we think God's existence is initially.

THEO: Huh? Explain please.

GENE: Okay, look at those rustling bushes over there. The fact that they're rustling raises the probability that there's a velociraptor lurking behind them, but you'd be a fool to jump up and run.

THEO: Of course you would. Those buddies can outrun you, no problem.

GENE: No, not just because of that. You'd be a fool to believe there was a velociraptor over there because your independent evidence tells you that any velociraptor's being alive in the twenty-first century is extremely unlikely. The rustling of the bushes makes it more likely since a velociraptor would likely make the bushes rustle. But no such observation could make it probable enough to believe. Similarly, you might, like Eva, give a very low probability assignment to the hypothesis that God exists, and the observation of fine-tuning would similarly fail to bring it to the point of believability.

EVA: Right. I mean, it would take a lot for me to believe that there was a supernatural entity of any sort, much less an all-powerful one. Talk about unlikely!

THEO: Not to me. Maybe my probability assignment for this is just higher.

GENE: Well, it's hard to pin down a notion of objective probability here, but that doesn't mean that you can assign whatever probability you want. There has to be some evidence—something that shows it's likely that God exists.

EVA: And that's precisely what we're trying to find. Given our evidence, it seems improbable that there's a spirit who can move mountains, much less create them.

GENE: It's hard for me to tell what exactly is likely in this context. That's part of the reason why I'm an agnostic.

EVA: I think you're just wishy-washy. But there's another problem with all of these design arguments, the fine-tuning argument included. I think it's the most serious problem of all, in fact.

THEO: What's that?

EVA: This whole argument is predicated upon the fact that we need to posit God to explain the fortuitous initial settings of the universe. But that's an explanation only if we can explain the fortuitous initial settings of God!

THEO: God isn't a microwave oven, Eva. What are you talking about?

EVA: Look. We're supposed to be brought to our explanatory knees by the claim that gosh, isn't it unlikely that there's a finely tuned universe? What are the chances? But the same thing can be said about God. Isn't it unlikely that there is this god with these particular life-favoring desires? I mean, what are the chances? Lucky for us there wasn't the god who loves the void, or the god who loves fire, fire, and more fire. What explains the fact that we were so lucky to draw this god?

THEO: There's no explaining that. It's just what God wants—it's part of His loving nature to want there to be people to experience joy and love.

GENE: Which is it? That there's no explanation or that the explanation is His nature?

THEO: It's His loving nature.

EVA: It really doesn't matter, because either answer gets you into trouble. If you say it's His nature, I'll just say, "How lucky that He has that nature! What explains that?" If you say there's no explanation, I can't help but wonder why you demand an explanation for the initial settings of the universe but not for the nature of your God? If one of us should have to provide such an explanation, then the other should too.

THEO: I think there are reasons to believe such questions can't, in principle, be asked about God's nature.

EVA: How's that supposed to work? Even if I buy that something needs to explain the way the universe is, how am I supposed to be satisfied if that explanation itself has no explanation?

THEO: I'm not saying there's no explanation. I'm saying only that the nature of God couldn't be other than it is. So, we can't really ask, "Why is He as He is?" or at least not in the same way we can ask about the universe.

GENE: Are we planning on making Chicago by nightfall?

THEO: Of course! Wait. What time is it?

GENE: Let's just say we'd better resume this conversation later.

EVA: Shotgun!

GENE: You're a child, Eva.

EVA: Shotgun, shotgun, shotgun!

GENE: Fine. Let's go.

4
Chicago, Illinois, outside the Adler Planetarium

The Cosmological Argument

It's nighttime in the Windy City. Theo, Eva, and Gene exit the planetarium and walk, somewhat dazed, to the north.

EVA: Wow.

THEO: You said it. Wow.

GENE: You gotta love a good planetarium.

EVA: Good? That was incredible!

THEO: Mind-boggling. Let's go again tomorrow.

GENE: Nope, tomorrow is the Art Institute. We have a schedule here, and it doesn't allow for encores.

EVA: I'm kinda surprised you liked it as much as you did, Theo.

THEO: Why? I love that stuff.

EVA: Well the universe depicted on the ceiling in there didn't exactly seem to have a lot of divine interventions. One explosion after another, that's how it seemed to me.

THEO: Oh, don't tell me we're back to this! Can't you leave this be?

GENE: You know the answer to that one, Theo. You asked for it, going on a road trip with a philosopher. What did you expect?

THEO: I'm a glutton for punishment.

EVA: So tell me. The cosmological story we just saw had no supernatural players. God made no appearance. What's more, life and humanity don't seem to occupy the central place presupposed by the arguments you were making earlier.

THEO: *Au contraire!*

GENE: Please tell me you didn't just say "*au contraire.*"

THEO: Indeed I did. What we saw in there only bolstered my sense that there's a divine being, the conductor for that cosmic symphony!

EVA: Oh, please. A conductor? It's not like any of those red dwarfs or black holes are going to hit a wrong note! It's all governed by the laws of nature!

THEO: Well, that might be, but something had to set everything in motion!

GENE: Is it just me, or have we had this conversation before?

THEO: This point is a little different.

EVA: Sounds suspiciously similar to me.

THEO: Similar, but not the same. Let's say I grant that we can't infer that God exists from the fact that life, the universe, and everything seem to have been designed.

EVA: Consider it said.

THEO: That doesn't mean that God isn't a necessary part of the equation.

GENE: Wait, once you've granted that life, the universe, and everything can exist without God, how could He be a necessary part of things?

THEO: I didn't grant *that*. I only granted that one can't legitimately infer that God exists from the appearance of design. One can, however, infer His existence from something else.

EVA: Which is…?

THEO: Something had to cause all of this to start happening! Something was needed to set everything in motion. The other arguments claim that God is the best explanation for some of the particularly elegant things we observe about our universe. Here I'm claiming that His existence is needed to explain how everything got started, regardless of the elegance and function we find in nature.

EVA: Ah, I see. That's called…

THEO: The Cosmological Argument. I think there's something to this one too.

EVA: So you can no doubt make the argument more explicit for us?

THEO: I think so. How about this:

1. Something exists.
2. Nothing can exist without being caused to exist.
3. Nothing causes itself to exist.
4. There can be no chain of causes extending infinitely into the past.
5. Therefore, there must have been a first cause.

EVA: Um, I think you're leaving something out. The bit about … who's that guy? Name starts with "G."

THEO: Very funny. Here's the rest:

6. That first cause was God.
7. If God ever existed, then He exists.
8. Therefore, God exists.

GENE: Well, that's better than your previous arguments in one sense: it doesn't make spurious inferences about what best explains particular features of the world.

EVA: Yeah, but its generality opens another weakness. Even if we grant your argument, we can't really conclude what Theo wants to conclude. We can't conclude, for example, that God is still around, that God is good or caring, or even that there's only one god. It's hard to see how we can infer much at all about this first cause of yours that even warrants our calling it "God." Premise 6 is unjustified.

THEO: Look, if I can prove there had to be a first cause of the universe, isn't that enough? Can't that be my good deed for the day?

GENE: Maybe, if you're willing to allow that your first cause is basically the dense speck of energy that precipitated the Big Bang.

THEO: Big Bang, big deal. Something has to have caused that!

GENE: Well, I'll bet there will be some very surprised cosmologists!

Eva: Wait a sec, Gene. I think there's a problem with the argument that might shed some light on your disagreement with Theo. The argument contradicts itself.

Theo: How do you figure?

Eva: Your second premise says that all existing things were caused to exist. If that's true, then how can there be a first cause? It can't cause itself, because that's ruled out by your third premise: nothing can cause itself to exist. Your argument seems actually to prove that God *can't* exist, at least if you construe him as a first cause.

Theo: Oops.

Gene: Yeah, that really isn't good.

Theo: Hold on now. I think this can be fixed pretty easily. I didn't mean everything has a cause. I meant everything natural has a cause.

Eva: You mean everything except for God. That's convenient.

Theo: No, it's not that simple. I meant to say that everything in nature is governed by natural law and so has a cause. We shouldn't expect this to hold for things outside of nature, like God himself.

Gene: Okay, so the new argument is…?

Theo: This:

1. There are things that exist in nature.
2. Everything that exists in nature was caused to exist.
3. Nothing in nature causes itself to exist.
4. There is no chain of causes extending infinitely into the past.
5. Therefore, there must have been a nonnatural first cause.
6. That nonnatural first cause was God.
7. If God ever existed, then He exists.
8. Therefore, God exists.

Gene: That does sound better.

Eva: Not much. Why think that everything in nature has a cause? Because everything in nature falls under natural law? If that's your reason, not only can you conclude that everything in nature has a cause, you can conclude that everything in nature has a *natural* cause! Once again, God is left out of the works.

THEO: I think our sense that everything natural has a cause goes deeper than that. There must be an explanation for why things are as they are, and only if things have causes is such an explanation available.

GENE: Uh, come again?

THEO: Consider everything we just saw in the planetarium: the entire science of cosmology is driven by our need to answer certain questions. Why does the Earth rotate around the sun? Why are the moon and the Earth made out of similar elements? Why is the sun so hot? Science is driven by the conviction that these questions must have answers. So, science is committed to premise 2: everything in nature was caused.

GENE: That sounds right, actually. In science, we assume that the way things are is explained by their causes.

EVA: The principle you guys have in mind seems to motivate inquiry across the board. It's sometimes called the Principle of Sufficient Reason. It has many formulations: every event must have a cause; there must be a full explanation for anything that's true; and there are other formulations. All of them basically come to the same thing: for every coherent question why, there must be a coherent answer. Many of the great philosophers took the Principle of Sufficient Reason as a basic truth.

GENE: Who, for example?

EVA: Lots of them. Leibniz is maybe the clearest example.

GENE: Leibniz? The guy who invented calculus?

THEO: I thought Issac Newton did that.

EVA: They both did. Independently. At the same time.

THEO: Huh.

EVA: Anyway, I'm not sure science is committed to any version of the Principle. For example, aren't there discoveries in quantum mechanics that suggest that some things lack causes?

GENE: That's true. It appears that some events, such as the decay of certain radioactive elements, are irreducibly indeterministic: there's no sufficient reason for the decay to happen when it does. More generally, particles sometimes randomly appear and sometimes randomly vanish. That's just how the universe works. At least, that view is widely accepted among physicists who think about such things. And this is hard science, not speculative philosophy.

THEO: Quantum mechanics! Whenever someone wants to explain something that makes no sense while retaining the appearance of scientific respectability, they just utter the words "quantum mechanics" and everyone is awestruck.

GENE: Sometimes it seems that way, I admit. But that's not what I'm doing. Specific experimental evidence backs up my claim: some quantum events are uncaused.

EVA: Are you sure? Why can't Theo, or anyone who wants to defend the premise that everything in nature is caused, say that there *is* a cause of these quantum events, we just don't know what it is?

THEO: Eva, on my side? It's an inexplicable miracle!

EVA: Enjoy it while it lasts.

THEO: Seriously, though, what she says sounds right: the evidence about quantum mechanics shows only that we don't know the causes of some events, or maybe that we can't know them.

GENE: Okay, I should backpedal a bit. There's disagreement about how to interpret the evidence, and the view you suggest fits with some interpretations. But other viable interpretations imply that there really are uncaused events. So, even if the existence of such events hasn't been definitively established, it's considered a serious possibility.

EVA: Well, my skepticism about the Principle of Sufficient Reason doesn't depend entirely on irreducible quantum indeterminacy anyway. There are other objections to the Principle.

THEO: Such as?

EVA: Well, the philosopher David Hume pointed out that there's nothing incoherent in the idea of something suddenly happening without a cause. For example, we can imagine a brick just blinking into existence and falling to the ground.

THEO: Yeah, we can imagine it, but so what? Things like that happen only in cartoons.

EVA: It's true, such things don't usually happen in reality. But when you're talking about the beginning of everything, you're hardly talking about usual circumstances. Even on your view something quite unusual happens in the beginning—something unnatural sets things in motion.

THEO: True.

Eva: I say all bets are off for the beginning of the universe. If we can coherently imagine something just popping into existence without a cause, then we can't rule it out as a possibility. And that doesn't seem less likely than the scenario in which an unknown supernatural being suddenly gives the universe a kick-start. We can't subscribe to the premise that everything in nature must have a cause just because that premise applies to things we're familiar with.

Gene: Yeah, but that premise still seems pretty compelling to me, Eva.

Eva: Well, that could be explained by the fact that everything you've ever experienced has a cause.

Gene: That could be. But even if I grant that premise, I don't think the argument works. I'd attack premise 4. Why think there's no chain of causes extending infinitely into the past?

Eva: I agree. I don't see any reason to buy that premise either.

Theo: You don't? How could things just go back forever?

Eva: I admit it's a little staggering to think about. But that doesn't mean it's incomprehensible, let alone false. What we just saw in the planetarium was staggering. I still can't get my head around the age of the Earth, much less the age of the universe. But that's a limit on my imagination, not on the nature of the world.

Theo: This seems different, though. It seems literally incomprehensible that the events of this moment stand at the end of an infinite chain of causes.

Gene: Anything involving infinity is pretty daunting, but I don't see why it's incomprehensible. You admit there's an infinite series of positive integers, right? One, two, three, and so on.

Theo: Sure.

Gene: And there's a parallel, backwards sequence of negative integers, right?

Theo: Right, but a sequence of numbers is different.

Gene: Just hold on a second. Why do you believe the negative sequence is infinite?

Theo: You recognize that for any number you choose, there's always a number that's one less.

GENE: Exactly. So call the current moment zero. There must be a moment before zero, right? And before that, and before that, and so on. For any moment, there must be a previous moment. If you can grasp the bit about numbers, you can grasp this.

THEO: I'm fine with that. I just don't see how natural causes can go back forever.

EVA: I don't see why not. Why can't you be born from your parents, and them from theirs, and your grandparents from their parents, and so on? Everyone has parents who account for their existence, and it doesn't seem impossible that this should go back forever. Of course it doesn't, because we have evidence that there was a time before there was any life. But it could have been that way.

GENE: Right. I mean, presently it looks like our story ends with the Big Bang. But there's nothing incoherent in imagining that the dense dot of energy at the Big Bang was a result of a contraction of a previous universe—a universe that itself once expanded from the explosion of a dense dot of energy. And so on and so forth, back forever. There's nothing incoherent there, right?

THEO: I don't know. Thinking about that hurts the brain.

EVA: And thinking about the idea of an infinite God—about what that might even mean—hurts *my* brain.

THEO: That's not surprising.

GENE: Because Eva's brain is sensitive?

THEO: No: because God is incomprehensible to us.

EVA: Aha! So the universe couldn't have extended back infinitely because such an infinite regress is incomprehensible, so it must have been caused by an infinite being—who is, by the way, incomprehensible?! Surely, something is off here.

GENE: I've got to agree with Eva here, Theo. You did a good job of saving your argument from incoherence by making your premises specific to natural things and events. But there's still the question as to why you're exempting God from the constraints you put on nature.

THEO: Well isn't it obvious that God is supernatural? Isn't it clear He's not subject to the same constraints as rocks and planets?

EVA: Once again, Theo, you've got to remember that you're trying to prove the existence of God. You aren't simply trying to incorporate Him into an otherwise naturalistic worldview. You can't come in with the assumption that there's a god that can't be held to the same standards as nature.

GENE: Right. If our search for the origin of the universe convinces us that something counterintuitive happens—either that something causes itself, that something appears uncaused, or that there's an infinite chain of causes—that gives us no reason to claim that this something must be supernatural.

EVA: Let me put it another way. Even though you've artificially exempted God from these questions in your argument, we can still ask, "What caused God?" If your answer is that nothing did, we can ask why He can come out of nothing while nothing else can. It seems like a double standard. If your answer is that God caused Himself, then we can ask why He can cause Himself and nothing else can.

THEO: I think the question just doesn't apply to God. God is eternal and has always existed.

EVA: So God's existence tails backwards infinitely? Why can God do that whereas nature can't? This is just another double standard.

GENE: Once again, if the reason you reject the possibility of an infinite chain of causes in nature is that you can't comprehend it, then it seems the same reason should lead you to reject the notion of an eternal god.

THEO: I think you guys are underestimating the sense in which God differs from things in the natural world. Look at it this way. Suppose I grant the possibility of an infinite chain of causes leading up to the present state of the world. I'll agree with you that each step of the chain is caused and explained by the previous step. But still, something needs to explain why the chain is there and why there's this chain and not another.

GENE: I don't follow. Why do we need to further explain the whole chain if every link is explained? The chain is nothing over and above the links!

THEO: Let's go back to the parenthood analogy. So I'm born of my parents, they're born of my grandparents, and so on back forever.

GENE: Right.

THEO: And for simplicity's sake, let's just focus on this, the Logan chain of ancestry.

GENE: Okay.

THEO: Now as it happens, I'm blond. This fact needs an explanation, which in this case happens to be that my parents are blond, all of my grandparents are—or were—blond, and so were my great grandparents.

EVA: Really? That's very unlikely.

THEO: Well, I'm simplifying for the sake of argument. But yeah, we're mostly blond. In any case, the reason each of us is blond has a full explanation in terms of genetics, right?

EVA: Right.

THEO: But it seems as though instead of this infinite chain of blonds, there could have been a different chain. I could have had brown hair, if one of my parents had different genes.

EVA: But that would require…

THEO: Yeah, I know, that would require that their parents had slightly different genes, and so on all the way down the line. My question is, why isn't this brunet line the actual one? And why is there a Logan line at all?

GENE: I'm not sure I get the question.

THEO: The general point is simple. Infinite chain or not, things could have been other than they are, right?

GENE: Right. Or at least I think so.

THEO: Okay, so why aren't they?

GENE: I still don't understand what you're asking.

THEO: Now you're just being stubborn. You know what I'm asking.

GENE: No, no I don't. I don't see what sort of explanation you're looking for.

EVA: I think I see…

THEO: Oh, thank God.

EVA: No, I think I see the Art Institute up ahead. Too bad it's closed. We could go tonight. I can't wait to see that Magritte exhibit.

GENE: How come every philosophy major I know likes Magritte? I don't get it. Just a bunch of spheres, bowlers, and mirrors.

THEO: Excuse me, weren't we having a conversation?

EVA: Sorry. What were you saying?

THEO: Basically, the idea was that if things could have been otherwise, we need an explanation of why they aren't. God is that explanation.

EVA: Okay, I think a little premise-conclusion form would be helpful here.

THEO: I thought you'd say that. So let's see...

1. Things could have been different: the universe might have been different than it is, or there might have been no universe at all.

2. Whenever things could have been different, there is something that explains why they are the way they are.

3. Therefore, there is something that explains why things are the way they are.

4. The best explanation of that is that God made them that way.

5. If that is the best explanation, then God exists.

6. Therefore, God exists.

GENE: Whoa there, Theo. Even if I bought your premises, you've really snuck God in at the end there, haven't you?

THEO: I suppose that might be a little quick.

EVA: I'll say. There are two big questions. First, why think that the explanation must be God, and second, what explains God?

THEO: I think I can answer both questions at once. Whatever explains why things are this way rather than that way must be something that couldn't be other than it is.

GENE: Why is that?

THEO: Well, unless we end in something that couldn't be other than it is, more explanation will be called for. In that case, we'd never get a complete explanation for why things are the way they are. We'll always just put it off to the next step.

GENE: I don't see why we need explanations like this. It just seems...

EVA: Hold on there, Gene. You're questioning premise 2. And premise 2 is another version of the Principle of Sufficient Reason. We've been over that.

GENE: True, though this one isn't exactly about everything having a cause.

EVA: Okay, fair enough. But first we should see if the argument can stand on its own feet.

THEO: What's your point, Eva?

EVA: That your argument needs another premise: one saying that the explanation of why things are the way they are must involve something that couldn't be otherwise. Right?

THEO: Fine. So now we have to ask what sort of a thing that could be.

GENE: Good question. I'd be inclined to say that nothing fits that description.

THEO: You think everything could be other than it is?

GENE: Why not? Everything I can think of seems like it could have been different. The Art Institute could have been made with an extra gallery for preschool art. The Wrigley Building could have been slightly less ornate. The Cubs could have won the World Series. With sufficient changes here and there, anything could have been different.

EVA: Actually, that's not so clear. Maybe some things couldn't have been otherwise. I mean, consider the number two. Could it have been different in some way?

GENE: Sure! We might have had three eyes, instead of two.

EVA: I mean the number two itself. Could *it* have been different? Could it have been composite instead of prime? Or could it have occupied a different place in the natural number sequence?

GENE: I suppose not. But these don't sound like the sorts of things that could explain the way things are. And they don't sound like God. I mean, those things exist but only in an abstract sense.

EVA: What exactly do you mean?

GENE: What I mean is concrete existence, as opposed to merely abstract existence. I admit that may sound wishy-washy. But you can see what I'm driving at, can't you? There are things like cars, clouds, and colors. Those are concrete. And then there are entities like numbers and abstract concepts. We don't want to model God after the number two or some abstract concept, do we?

THEO: I think that's right. God is more concrete than those things, even if He's not concrete in the way physical objects are.

GENE: Right. And anything with concrete existence can be imagined to be other than it actually is, no? Any concrete thing I can imagine existing I can also imagine failing to exist. See that grotesque building ahead of us?

THEO: Grotesque? That's the Pritzker Pavilion. It's a famous piece by Frank Gehry!

GENE: Famous or not, yuck.

EVA: I kind of like it, actually. Looks sort of like a big metal ribbon. It's festive.

GENE: I suppose it's nice that you and Theo can agree on something. Anyway, there it is, larger than life, but I can imagine—or even wish— that it didn't exist. Just imagine that the city of Chicago got cold feet at the last moment, before construction began.

EVA: I think we get your point. Hume thought the same thing, and I guess I tend to agree.

THEO: Anyway, Eva, once again you're making a point about the powers of the imagination. I don't see what follows from the fact that you can't imagine something. That may be just a limitation of your imagination.

EVA: Well first of all, Theo, all we have to go on here is what we can conceive or imagine. Your argument isn't going to be persuasive if you promise us that despite the fact that we can't imagine it, God is a being that couldn't be other than He is. Second, you yourself are relying on the accuracy of your imagination in premise 1, when you say that the universe could be other than it is.

GENE: That's right, Theo. By saying that, aren't you admitting that every concrete thing you can think of might not have existed? And aren't you basing that on the fact that you can imagine any such thing not existing?

THEO: I do think that's true of every concrete thing except God.

GENE: It really is remarkable how God proves the constant exception to your rules. I'm inclined to say that if we can't come up with any other examples of concrete things that have to be as they are, we shouldn't think God is any different.

THEO: Unless, of course, there's an argument that He must be different.

GENE: Fine, I'll grant that. But I doubt there's any such an argument.

THEO: Actually, there is…

EVA: Hold on a second. Let's refocus. You say, Theo, we've got to assume God exists to explain how the world is the way it is, right?

THEO: Right.

EVA: And to do such explaining, God has to be such that (a) He can't fail to exist and (b) He can't be other than He is.

THEO: Right.

EVA: Well, even granting that we can understand what you mean by that, I wonder whether you're really getting what you want.

THEO: If I can have God, that's enough for me.

EVA: What I'm wondering is whether what you'll have is anything like what most people think of as God. For example, if God can't be other than He is, He doesn't sound all-powerful. More importantly, it doesn't sound like He's even free.

THEO: Hmm. I think I see what you mean.

GENE: Why wouldn't God be free?

EVA: Because He couldn't be other than He is! That means, among other things, that He couldn't do otherwise. He couldn't act in any way other than how He does in fact act. Think of it this way. Suppose we say God accounts for the way things are because He chose them to be this way.

THEO: That's exactly what I'm saying.

EVA: But of course that can't be the end of the story, because now we have to ask: why did He choose in that way? Once we can ask that question, we no longer have the end of our explanation, unless of course He couldn't have chosen any other way.

GENE: So in that case He's not free.

EVA: Right. Though to be honest, debates about freedom get messy. In any case, it doesn't look good for theism if God is constrained in this way.

GENE: I see. Actually, the situation looks even worse than that.

THEO: A God that isn't free looks pretty bad already.

GENE: But suppose that God must exist and that He couldn't act other than He did, so He had to create things as they are.

THEO: Right.

GENE: Then it turns out that your initial supposition in premise 1 is false! The universe couldn't actually be other than it is!

EVA: Yeah, that is worse. It looks, in fact, like you've got a dilemma on your hands.

THEO: Oh, I hate having dilemmas on my hands. They're harder to get off than Duncan's blood. So what's this alleged dilemma?

EVA: Either God is free to make things differently than He made them or He isn't.

THEO: I'm with you so far.

EVA: If He's free to make things differently, then His decision to make things as they are can't explain what needs explaining.

THEO: Why not?

EVA: Because now His choice itself needs explaining. So, then God is not, in fact, the ultimate explanation you're looking for and your argument fails.

GENE: Okay, that's one horn of the dilemma. What's the other?

EVA: If God isn't free to make things differently, then not only do you lose the idea of a God that can act freely, but you contradict your initial premise that the universe could have been different than it is.

GENE: That's a dilemma, all right. Ready to give up on this argument, Theo?

THEO: Well, I admit it doesn't look good. But I'm not sure the second horn of the dilemma is so bad. Suppose I admit that in some sense God isn't free, and that He had to—perhaps because of His nature—create the world as it is. Then it's true that the world couldn't be different than it is, but so what? Why can't I accept that?

EVA: Well, it seems you're basically saying it's an illusion that things could have been different than they are, right? It really was possible that anyone other than Jeffrey Johnson won the lottery.

THEO: Who's Jeffrey Johnson?

EVA: Jeffrey Johnson is an example. So am I right? That's what you're saying, Theo?

THEO: Right.

EVA: So it seems that if you're going to wind up with that view, your opponents can start out saying the same thing, thus denying your first premise—the premise that things could have been different.

THEO: But I arrived at the claim that things couldn't have been different by reflecting on the implications of God's nature. Nontheists don't have similar grounds for making the same claim.

GENE: Wait a minute, Theo. So far you haven't provided a single explanation of why God is the only candidate for a necessary being. And suppose you come up with reasons to conclude God is a necessary being. To make your argument work, you'll need to show that those reasons don't apply to any natural thing. I see no reason to think that can be done.

EVA: Yeah, Theo, I have to say this argument doesn't look any better than the last. In general, for any of your arguments to work you're going to have to hold nature to some requirement while giving God a free pass on that requirement. Again, the double standard.

THEO: Okay, maybe so. I'm certainly tired of arguing the point. Our hotel's just across the street, after all. Still, explain this to me. What, exactly, do you guys say about the beginning of the universe? In my view, it was started by God. What's your view?

GENE: I don't have a view. I don't really see any evidence that would lead me to take a position on the matter. There are various possibilities, I suppose, but unless strong scientific evidence points in one direction over another, I see no more reason to commit on this than on the number of stars in the sky.

EVA: I pretty much agree. I probably have some inclination to think that nature involves a chain of causes that extends back forever. Who knows, though? It could be that this is an issue that will just be shrouded in mystery forever. That wouldn't surprise me.

THEO: Well, this is certainly an odd resolution. I mean, you guys have spent the last hour or so arguing against the view that God started the universe.

GENE: Time flies.

EVA: Time them doing what?

THEO: Hey, knock it off. I'm serious. You guys just pile on the criticisms of the view that God started it all. But now when I ask you for your own views you throw up your hands and say, "Beats me! It's a mystery!"

GENE: Theo, we weren't arguing that God didn't start things up. We were arguing that there's insufficient evidence that He did, and thus that there's no argument here for the existence of God.

EVA: An example might help explain our stance. Suppose you were missing the keys to your car, and I said a pickpocket took them, simply because I saw them dangling from your pocket earlier. You and Gene would be right to criticize me for concluding that a pickpocket took them, or even that there was a pickpocket in the planetarium at all, based solely on that evidence. Your criticisms would be valid even if, when I asked you what you thought happened to the keys, you both shrugged and said you didn't know.

GENE: Right. In fact, it would be perfectly reasonable for us to believe that there was no pickpocket even if we didn't know what happened to the keys. Another explanation might be much more likely.

THEO: Hey, guys. Where are my keys? They're not in my pocket!

GENE: Must have been a pickpocket!

EVA: Or a gremlin. We mustn't discount the gremlin hypothesis.

THEO: Really, where are they? We've got to go back…

EVA: Here they are, bonehead. They fell out of your pocket in the planetarium.

THEO: I hate you guys.

GENE: See how easy these things can be?

THEO: C'mon guys. Let's go grab a beer and see some jazz. We're in Chicago, after all. We can't spend all our time arguing.

GENE: Now *there's* an argument I can get behind!

EVA: I'm in. Let's take a cab. Cars are so Ohio.

5
Chicago, Illinois, in the Hotel

The Ontological Argument

Theo and Gene are in a room with the curtains pulled. Theo is kicking back on one of the double beds, reading, while Gene has his head covered with a pillow.

THEO: You can't stay asleep all day, you know. Eva's on her way over.

GENE: Mmmmfh!

THEO: It's really a waste, you know, being in Chicago and spending half the day with a pillow over your head. You're going with us to the Art Institute, right?

GENE: Mmmfh.

There is a knock on the door. Theo gets up to answer it.

EVA: Rise and shine, sleepyheads! It's a beautiful day in the Windy City!

THEO: It is?

EVA: Not really. It's a little rainy, actually. Nothing that will stop us, though, right, Gene?

GENE: Mmmfh.

THEO: Gene's still feeling a bit rough from last night.

EVA: I warned him about those Jell-O shots. Those things are pure gelatinous disaster.

THEO: Yeah, he was pretty inspired last night. Weren't you, Gene?

GENE: Mmmfh.

EVA: Let's at least open up these curtains and let some light in here. This place is depressing. By the way, have you guys eaten?

THEO: Nope. We were, or rather I was, waiting for you. Wanna go grab something? Gene, you up for that?

GENE: Nnnmf.

EVA: Is that a no?

THEO: I've come to interpret that as a no. Want to just order room service? It's expensive, but I'm feeling lazy.

EVA: You paying?

THEO: Of course. Have you paid for anything yet on this trip?

EVA: Just checking. Order me a tuna sandwich.

THEO: Tuna, check. Gene?

GENE: Mmmf.

THEO: I'll get him some fries.

Theo places the order and flops himself into a recliner in the corner.

THEO: Ten minutes, they said.

EVA: Good, I'm starving. Listen, do you remember saying yesterday that you thought God was the one thing that had to exist and that couldn't be any different than He is?

THEO: Yep.

EVA: You weren't thinking of the Ontological Argument, were you?

THEO: Actually, I was.

EVA: Do you actually think that's a good argument for the existence of God?

THEO: To be honest, I go back and forth. Sometimes it seems just miserable, but other times it can seem quite persuasive.

EVA: I'm familiar with the first times, but not the second. Care to try to convince me otherwise?

THEO: I guess. It doesn't look like we're going to get to the Art Institute anytime soon.

EVA: Alright, shoot. If you convert me with this argument, I'll tow the car the rest of the way to California with my teeth.

THEO: I won't count on it, but it's worth trying just to keep that image in my mind for a little while. Okay, so you know St. Anselm's version of the argument?

EVA: I haven't thought about it since Intro. Refresh my memory.

THEO: As it happens, I was just reading about it in one of the books you brought along. So, you know, Anselm is trying to refute the fool who doesn't believe in God.

EVA: Right. Where "fool" means "atheist." Subtle. Anyway, if I recall, Anselm has a sort of awkward description of God.

THEO: It sounds awkward, but I think it makes sense: God is that than which nothing greater can be conceived.

EVA: Right. That's a tongue twister.

THEO: Yeah, but the idea is just that God is the greatest.

EVA: The greatest what?

THEO: The greatest conceivable being. If you think you can conceive of something greater than God, then you're just confused.

EVA: Greater in what sense?

THEO: Well, that's debatable, but let's say He's at least the most worthy of awe and worship.

EVA: I'm not sure that helps me, but go on.

THEO: Okay, so let's say in this case that you're the fool.

EVA: Ha ha.

THEO: Well if the shoe fits… In any case, Anselm says this:

> …even the fool is bound to agree that there is at least in the understanding something than which nothing greater can be imagined, because when he hears this he understands it, and whatever is understood is in the understanding. And certainly that than which nothing greater can be imagined cannot be in the understanding alone. For if it is at least in the understanding alone, it can be imagined to be in reality too, which is greater.

Therefore if that than which a greater cannot be imagined is in the understanding alone, that very thing than which a greater cannot be imagined is something than which a greater can be imagined. But certainly this cannot be. There exists, therefore, beyond doubt something than which a greater cannot be imagined, both in the understanding and in reality. (Anselm)

Eva: Whew!

Theo: I know. You should try reading it out loud. It's a peck of pickled peppers.

Eva: So can you give me the CliffsNotes on that one?

Theo: I'll try. The reasoning is basically that since God is the greatest conceivable being, He can't be just an idea, because you can conceive of something greater than that—namely a real thing that the idea represents. So, God must exist.

Eva: I'm not sure how much that helped. It seems like a conceptual shell game. Maybe it will clarify things if you...

Theo: Put things in premise-conclusion form? How did I guess? Okay, here we go.

1. There is, in the understanding at least, a being than which nothing greater can be conceived.

2. If that being exists only in the understanding, then it's possible to conceive of something greater, namely the same being except existing in reality as well as in the understanding. This is a contradiction since you're now *conceiving of something greater* than the *greatest conceivable* being.

3. Therefore, that being does not exist only in the understanding.

4. If that being does not exist only in the understanding, it exists in reality.

5. Therefore, God, a being than which nothing greater can be conceived, exists in reality.

6. Therefore, God exists.

Got that?

Eva: I think so. Okay, let me see. So let's start with premise 1: a being than which nothing greater can be conceived exists at least in the understanding.

THEO: Right.

EVA: So, even I must admit that the *idea* of God exists in my head, since that idea is part of the thought I think when I deny God exists?

THEO: Right.

EVA: Hmmm. And since anything I can imagine can exist, and God actually existing would be greater than God simply being an idea in my mind, He must exist.

THEO: Right.

EVA: Ooh. That's as bad as I remember it being. How can such a stinker of an argument have been so influential?

THEO: Hold on now. I don't think it's as bad as all that. What's wrong with it?

EVA: Well, for one thing, the first premise is obviously false!

There is a knock on the door.

BELLHOP: Room Service!

EVA: Excellent.

Eva runs and opens the door. A large man in a polyester suit wheels a tray into the room, and Theo signs the bill.

EVA: Excuse me sir, but do you think there's something than which nothing greater can be conceived?

BELLHOP: I don't know. Maybe having a job where I don't have to interact with the guests of this hotel?

EVA: Oh.

BELLHOP: Have a good afternoon.

The bellhop leaves. Eva is aghast.

EVA: Did you tip him?

THEO: Of course.

EVA: You really shouldn't have tipped him. His quip was very rude.

THEO: I thought it was pretty clever. Anyway, you were saying?

EVA: Right, premise 1 is awful! It doesn't follow from the fact that I understand something that there's a place called the understanding where that thing is lurking! Nor does it follow from the fact that I imagine something that there's a place called the imagination where that thing is located.

THEO: Well, no, not in the literal sense in which we're presently located in Illinois.

EVA: Right. My imagination, if it's anywhere, is in my mind. I can imagine a rocket-powered goose, but there's no goose of any sort in my mind. There's maybe a concept of a goose, or an idea of a goose, but no goose.

THEO: Actually, that seems right to me.

EVA: Good. I think a lot of myself, as you're fond of pointing out. But even I don't think there's anything in my mind that's greater than anything anyone can conceive. This tuna sandwich, for example, seems greater than almost anything in my mind at the moment.

THEO: This burger is definitely better than any of your ideas at the moment.

EVA: Okay, then. Premise 2 looks false to me as well.

THEO: The one that says that the atheist would have to be able to conceive of something *greater than the greatest* conceivable being?

EVA: Right. That premise presupposes that we can conceive of a single thing that can exist both in my mind and as a concrete object in the world outside my mind. That doesn't seem right. Concepts and ideas are what are in the mind. What's it like to run into one of those when you're walking down the street?

THEO: That's fair. But think of it this way. Your ideas, which are in your mind, can always represent something in the world. At least, the ideas that make sense have that feature. So, say you have an idea of a winged horse. That idea exists in your understanding. Maybe Anselm's presupposition is just that, as long as there's nothing incoherent in that idea, it follows a winged horse could actually exist—not just in your mind, but in the real world.

EVA: Okay, that's plausible enough. But premise 2 still seems indefensible. There's no contradiction in saying both that the *idea* of a perfect being exists and that *what that idea represents* does not. It just doesn't follow from the fact that we have a representation of something that the thing represented exists, no matter how splendid the representation.

THEO: But Anselm's point is that in this case the represented thing must exist, because otherwise God wouldn't be greater than the idea of God—which is absurd.

EVA: But that's just a confusion. Think of it this way. Having a representation of something being a certain way doesn't imply that it really *is* that way. So, having a representation of something as being so great that it must exist doesn't imply that it, or anything else, is that way in reality.

THEO: I'm still not quite convinced.

EVA: Okay, suppose I have a dream in which Elvis appears in my bedroom. In the dream, I'm astonished and I ask him whether he's real. He answers, "Of course I'm real, honey. I'm The King! Thank you very much." That doesn't mean he's real. We might say he's real-in-my-dream, but he still doesn't really exist, outside my dream world.

THEO: Elvis fan that I am, I'm not sure these cases are the same.

EVA: I don't need Elvis.

THEO: Hold on there: we all need Elvis.

EVA: No, I mean I can put the point in a different way. On one way of understanding Anselm, he starts with the premise that God is perfect—and he infers that God's nature or essence includes actual existence.

THEO: Okay.

EVA: But that's not right. If we're careful, the "God is perfect" idea only gets Anselm something like this premise: *If* God exists, then He has all perfections, including actual existence. And that's compatible with God's *not* existing.

GENE: Mmmfh!

THEO: Maybe Gene disagrees. You want some fries, Gene? Make you feel better.

GENE: Nnnfh!

EVA: That's the sound that means, "no," right?

THEO: I'm operating on that assumption. You know, I basically agree with your criticisms of Anselm's argument.

EVA: You do?

THEO: Basically. I'm surprised you haven't mentioned the island.

EVA: Island?

THEO: One of the famous first replies to this argument was made by a monk named Gaunilo. He said that Anselm's argument must be unsound since using the same reasoning you could prove the existence of many things we know don't exist.

EVA: Ah, I do remember. He said we can just as easily imagine a perfect island, with monkey butlers, air conditioned caverns and coconuts filled with piña coladas, and by the same reasoning it must exist. It exists at least in our minds, but if it only existed in our minds it wouldn't be the perfect island because a real island would be better. So our perfect island must exist.

THEO: I'm not sure Gaunilo mentioned the monkey butlers, but yeah, that was basically his parody of Anselm's reasoning.

EVA: It does suggest that something must be wrong here. I told you the argument stunk.

THEO: But your criticisms don't pinpoint the error. You haven't diagnosed the problem.

EVA: I thought I did.

THEO: Well, perhaps. In fact, the most famous diagnosis is related to your second point. Kant's answer to Anselm was that "existence" isn't a predicate.

EVA: He's right. It's not a predicate. It's a subject.

THEO: No, no, Kant wasn't making a grammatical point. It's rather that Anselm seems to be claiming that a being *with* the property of existence is better than one *without* that property. Since God is the greatest conceivable being, He must therefore exist. Kant's point is that existence isn't a feature of things, like size, color, or shape. Features of things are ways things are or could be. Existence isn't a *way* something is or could be. Existence is the *being* part.

EVA: But we do sometimes talk about existence as though it were a property. For example, isn't existence something I have and Santa Claus lacks?

THEO: It's true that you exist and Santa doesn't. But that doesn't mean that existence is a property. Let me give you an example. This one doesn't involve Elvis.

EVA: Too bad. Go ahead, though.

THEO: Suppose I place a personals ad.

EVA: Have you ever done that?

THEO: No. Just suppose. And suppose I write in my ad that I'm a single white male searching for a dark-haired women who's intelligent and petite in stature.

Eva: That sounds like me!

Theo: I said intelligent.

Eva: Ha!

Theo: Also, suppose I specify that she should have a tattoo on her right earlobe and believe that Christ is her savior.

Eva: Well that does rule me out, but I don't know.... Are you trying to tell me something, Theo?

Theo: Yes, I'm trying to tell you about Kant's argument. So, suppose I also added, "Mustn't smoke, but must exist."

Eva: Well, that last bit would be a waste of your money.

Theo: Exactly! All of the other characteristics I listed are features that would rule someone in or out of my specification. Existence doesn't do that. No one fails that test.

Eva: What about Santa?

Theo: Well, it's true to say, "Santa Claus doesn't exist." But is there a being who is Santa Claus?

Eva: No.

Theo: So there isn't anyone who fails that test, is there?

Eva: I get what you're saying. Still, I don't know. I certainly think I'm glad to have the property of existence! So I guess I'm not sure existence isn't a property. But suppose it's not. How does that help explain where Anselm's argument goes wrong?

Theo: His argument requires the idea that God would be greater if He existed. Only properties of a thing can make it better or worse. So if existence isn't a property, it can't play the role Anselm needs it to play.

Eva: Hmm. This is pretty slippery.

Theo: Okay, I admit that's a little hard to grasp. Let me give you another example. Imagine a pumpkin.

Eva: Okay.

Theo: Now, imagine that same pumpkin existing.

Eva: Um, okay.

Theo: Now, have you imagined anything different?

Eva: Well, I imagined the pumpkin set in a field this time as opposed to imagining it just on its own.

THEO: Is it in an existent field or a nonexistent field? It had better be an existent field if you're imagining that the pumpkin exists.

EVA: Um, I'm kinda losing my bearings here, but suppose it's an existent field.

THEO: Okay, I'd like you to imagine the same field and pumpkin, except this time not existing.

EVA: I think I see what you're saying. Imagining an *existent* pumpkin might not differ so much from simply imagining *a pumpkin*.

THEO: Right. In fact, these acts of imagination are one and the same.

EVA: Okay, so applied to this example, Kant's point becomes a claim about ideas and imagination rather than about existence and properties.

THEO: You could put it that way.

EVA: How does all this affect Anselm's argument again?

THEO: It undermines his second premise, where Anselm derives a contradiction in the atheist's position. He implies there that you have two ideas, one of God *existing* and another of just plain God, the former being the greater of the two. If there's no difference between those ideas—if imagining God existing is the same as imagining God—then his argument doesn't fly.

EVA: Where does Anselm say that the atheist has two ideas, one of God and one of God existing? Doesn't he say rather that God-in-reality is greater than God-in-the-understanding?

THEO: On Anselm's view, even the atheist must concede that she can imagine God. But she must be able to imagine something greater as well—which, says Anselm, leads to contradiction. But if there's no difference between imagining one and imagining the other, then the atheist hasn't contradicted herself at all.

EVA: You've obviously thought a lot about this.

THEO: Yeah, actually I've been reading a biography of Anselm. Did you know he was exiled from England when he was the Archbishop of Canterbury?

EVA: No, I didn't. Was it because his arguments stunk?

THEO: I don't think that consideration was foremost on the King's mind.

EVA: If I had been the Queen, that's why I'd have exiled him.

THEO: Well then Anselm is just one more person who can be glad that you were never a monarch.

Gene stirs.

THEO: He lives!

GENE: Barely. What's that about Eva being a monarch?

EVA: It was just a joke. How are you feeling?

GENE: How do I look?

EVA: You look green. Have some French fries. They might help settle your stomach.

GENE: Thanks. So what are you guys droning on about? I think you were giving me nightmares.

THEO: We're talking about the ontological argument.

GENE: Now I do feel like I'm going to be sick.

EVA: Really? Don't turn towards me!

GENE: Not really. I just remember thinking that argument was pretty bad. Problems with a perfect island, right?

THEO: Good memory.

EVA: If that argument is so bad, how come people still talk about it?

THEO: Well, there's a version of it that's not so bad after all.

GENE: I suppose I'll have to hear about it if I want any more fries.

EVA: I certainly want to hear about it. Any medic who can patch up this soldier deserves respect!

THEO: This version has roots in some of Anselm's writings, including his reply to Gaunilo, but it's been revived and refined by contemporary philosophers. It ties in, actually, to what we were talking about last night. Remember how I was saying that God had to exist of necessity?

GENE: I remember talking about that, but I don't recall your making an argument for that claim.

THEO: Well, the claim is widely accepted among theologians. And there's good reason for that. If God existed contingently, then His existence would depend on the way things turned out—on luck, or in any case on something other than Himself. But God, as a perfect being, simply does *not* depend on other things. God is a being that depends on nothing but Himself.

Eva: I don't know, that seems suspicious. Why does perfection require complete independence?

Theo: Well, that's really not what the improved ontological argument is about. Can we just assume for now that God is by definition a necessary being? That has to exist if does exist?

Eva: Okay, let's see where that leads us.

Gene: Well, of course He has to exist if He exists. I have to exist if I exist. It's a contradiction to think otherwise!

Theo: No, what I mean is that if God exists, then it's impossible that He would have failed to exist. You're not like that. You do exist, but you didn't have to exist—your parent's might never have met.

Eva: So you're saying that, unlike me, God is a necessary existent: if he exists, he exists necessarily.

Theo: Exactly. By the very definition of God.

Gene: I still don't know about this.

Eva:. Perhaps it will help if we adopt a little philosophical terminology.

Gene: Oh yeah, that always helps.

Eva: Sarcasm noted. Philosophers often talk about ways the world could have been as "possible worlds." Possible worlds are alternative scenarios in which something is different. So, talking this way, there's a possible world where I didn't come on this trip, and a possible world where you didn't have any Jell-O shots last night.

Gene: Ah, to be in that world.

Eva: Those are two possible worlds, but any possibility is another world or part of one. There are no possible worlds, though, where round squares dance.

Gene: That's a relief. Just thinking about dancing round squares is making me queasy.

Theo: People don't actually believe these possible worlds are real, do they?

Eva: Actually, some do. The alternatives are surprisingly hard to defend. There's a sizable literature on this.

Gene: Sounds like philosophers need more to do. Good thing you're going to grad school.

Eva: At least I have a career plan. Anyway, the majority view is that the business about possible worlds is just a way of talking, a sort of cosmological metaphor.

Theo: Okay, so in your terminology, if God exists, He exists in all possible worlds—unlike you who exist, but don't exist in a world where your parents never met.

Eva: Okay, so what's the revamped ontological argument?

Theo: Well, now, I'll help myself to a premise you and Gene have been pushing on me in the past several days. You know how you've argued that if we can imagine or conceive of something, it's possible? You used that premise when arguing against the claim that everything had to have a cause. You said you could imagine a brick just appeared, uncaused, out of thin air, and so it was possible some things aren't caused.

Eva: Right. We did use that premise.

Theo: Okay, now it seems that you must be able to conceive of God's existing. Otherwise, it's not clear that you'd even understand what you're saying when you deny that He exists.

Gene: I'll grant that.

Eva: I'm a little worried about that, but for the sake of argument…

Theo: So, using your own premise, since you can conceive of God's existing, God might have existed. Or to put it in your terms, there's a possible world in which God exists.

Gene: Sure, anything's possible.

Eva: No, some things aren't possible. Remember the round squares?

Gene: Okay, but God's existence is at least possible. That assumption seems safe.

Eva: Again, I'll grant it for the sake of argument.

Theo: So, God exists in at least one possible world. But if He exists in that world, He must exist in all possible worlds.

Gene: Right.

Eva: Uh-oh.

Theo: And our world—the actual world—is a possible world.

Gene: Wait. This world isn't a possible world. It's the real world.

Eva: No, he's right, Gene. To say a world is a possible world is just to say it's not impossible. But clearly this world isn't impossible. It's actual, so it has to be possible! It's not *merely* a possible world, since it's actual. But it's a possible world nonetheless.

THEO: Okay, so this is a possible world. And we agreed that if God exists in some possible world, He exists in all possible worlds. It follows that He exists in this world. In other words, God exists!

EVA: I admit, that argument is interesting.

THEO: Don't tell me, tell Alvin Plantinga.

EVA: Okay, I'll tell him next time I see him.

GENE: Who?

EVA: He's a prominent theistic philosopher.

GENE: You know him personally?

EVA: Not yet, but I intend to network. Who you know matters in philosophy as much as anywhere. My logic TA warned me about this. He knows nobody.

THEO: So have I convinced you? Are you going to be pulling us to California with your teeth?

GENE: What?

EVA: It's a bet we made. No, Theo, I don't buy the argument.

THEO: What? You bought every premise!

GENE: You did, Eva. Looks like you'd better polish up those chompers.

THEO: Surely you think the conclusion follows from the premises.

EVA: Actually, I'm not sure. It would help to have them…

THEO: Written out in premise-conclusion form? Already done.

GENE: Wow. Did you wake up early this morning and prepare for this discussion?

THEO: Well, yeah.

GENE: You bum.

THEO: It's better than spending the morning with my head under a pillow.

GENE: Good point.

THEO: Thank you. The argument has two parts. The first establishes God's possibility, and the second infers His actuality. Here's the first part:

1. It's conceivable that God exists.
2. If it's conceivable that God exists, then it's possible that He exists.

3. Therefore, it's possible that God exists. In other words, there's at least one possible world in which He exists.

GENE: Okay.

THEO: And here's part two:

4. If it's possible that God exists, then it's necessary that He exists. In other words, if He exists in any possible world, then He exists in all possible worlds—including the actual world.

5. Therefore, God exists in the actual world. In other words, God exists.

GENE: I think there's a little verbal magic going on here.

EVA: I think you're probably right, Gene, but the argument looks pretty good. The premises seem to make sense, and the conclusion seems to follow from them.

THEO: If you think there's some sleight of hand, tell me where it is.

GENE: Well, you guys said you've already discussed the idea of the perfect island. I wonder if the same objection applies here. Why couldn't we define a perfect island as a wonderful island that exists in all possible worlds? Then it would seem that we could run the same argument for that.

EVA: Right. So we can call the perfect island Islandia, and define Islandia as the ideal island, with beaches and monkey butlers and all the rest of it, but also stipulate that it's an island that must exist in all possible worlds if it exists at all. It seems that we can conceive of Islandia existing, even if we don't think it exists in this world. But now the same reasoning applies: since we can conceive of it, it must exist in some world. But if it exists in any world, by definition it must exist in all of them. So it must exist in the actual world in particular. But that's absurd, so we know something's wrong with the argument.

THEO: I don't think the island objection works here.

GENE: Why not?

THEO: Your Islandia isn't really conceivable!

EVA: Oh that's convenient.

THEO: Look, if you think about it, an island isn't the sort of thing that can exist in all possible worlds. Think of the repercussions. There have got to be possible worlds without water or liquid of any kind. How could those worlds have islands? If Islandia exists in all possible worlds, then there are no completely dry possible worlds. But surely some such worlds are possible.

GENE: I see what you're saying, but why think it isn't just as absurd in the case of God?

THEO: Because it doesn't seem that imagining a God who exists in all worlds has the same problems. Here the repercussions aren't so bad. There are still worlds where things are quite different and where different things exist. It's only that none of those worlds fails to contain God. I see no parallel problems here.

EVA: Huh. Good point.

THEO: Thank you. Also, remember, I had an argument for why God has to exist in every world: it's because otherwise He would be dependent on something for His existence. Your argument for a perfect island isn't motivated in the same way.

EVA: I have to concede, this argument is interesting. I think it probably does force the atheist to change her stance.

THEO: You're kidding! You're ready to convert?

EVA: I said the atheist has to change her stance, not that she has to admit defeat.

THEO: Okay, so what's the deal?

EVA: Some atheists allow that God might have existed. I even granted that earlier, for the sake of argument. This version of the ontological argument shows that I can't do that.

GENE: Wow. Now the atheist position isn't looking so hot. Surely even you have to admit God is possible!

THEO: Yeah, Eva. The atheist position now looks like it claims too much.

EVA: Not really. The atheist says God doesn't exist. That's always been the basic position, and that hasn't changed. What Theo's argument shows is that God not only doesn't exist: He couldn't have existed. So, the same old atheist claim, using the same old reasoning, now has stronger implications—but only because the theist defines God as a necessary being.

THEO: Well, first of all, I didn't just insist that God is a necessary being. I argued for that conclusion. There's a difference, in case you hadn't heard.

EVA: Point taken.

THEO: Also, I still haven't heard the "same old" atheist reasoning you mentioned. What's the argument for atheism? So far all you've done is shoot down my arguments. But refuting arguments for theism doesn't show that God doesn't exist. So, what are you talking about?

EVA: We've actually seen hints of the argument already. This just doesn't look like a world with a divine creator. There's the panda's thumb and examples like that. There are also genocides and painful diseases.

THEO: There are answers to that sort of argument.

EVA: I'm sure there are, and I'll bet we'll talk about them in due course. But I have more to say about the improved ontological argument. I said that the atheist has no problem accepting the implication that God exists in every possible world if He exists in any. But actually, it's better than that. This move makes the argument for atheism a bit easier.

GENE: How's that?

EVA: Well, before Theo drew out that implication, the atheist had fewer resources. She had to base her argument on facts about the actual world, such as its shoddy construction. But now all she needs to show is that there's *some* possible world in which God doesn't exist, and her work is done.

GENE: Ah, I get it. So really, you're turning the theist's cleverness against himself.

EVA: Right. We now have a really easy argument against God's existence:

1. It's conceivable that God doesn't exist.
2. If it's conceivable that God doesn't exist, then it's possible that He doesn't exist.
3. Therefore, it's possible that God doesn't exist. In other words, there's at least one possible world in which He doesn't exist.
4. If it's possible that God doesn't exist, then it's necessary that He doesn't exist. In other words, if there is any possible world in which God doesn't exist, then He doesn't exist in any possible world—including the actual world.
5. Therefore, God does not exist in the actual world. In other words, God does not exist.

THEO: I should have known this is how things would go.

GENE: Yeah, and that argument looks pretty strong. I mean, out of the infinite number of different possible worlds, surely one is God-less.

THEO: That's not obvious at all. There might be worlds in which people have evidence that God does not exist. In those worlds, atheism might be a reasonable position. But even so, God exists in those worlds. He just doesn't make His existence known.

EVA: I don't know, Theo, I agree with Gene here. The anti-God version of the improved ontological argument looks better than the pro-God version.

GENE: I wouldn't say that. I think there's got to be at least one possible world in which God exists. So, the two versions are equally convincing.

EVA: If they are, then that's enough to neutralize the ontological argument. But actually, Gene, what you've said is inconsistent, given Theo's necessary-being conception of God.

GENE: How so? I'm not saying that there's any single world in which God both exists and doesn't exist. That would be inconsistent. All I'm saying is that there's one world in which God exists and another, different world in which He doesn't.

EVA: Those Jell-O-shots must have a long half-life.

THEO: She's right, Gene. When it comes to possible worlds, God's existence is an all-or-nothing affair. Either He exists in all possible worlds, or He exists in none. So, if there's one in which He exists, then there isn't any other in which He doesn't.

GENE: Oh, right, that makes sense. But wait a minute. I thought we all agreed that if we can conceive of something—if we can imagine it—then it's possible.

EVA: Actually, there are some potential counterexamples.

GENE: I'm sure there are, but let's not digress. Imagination is at least a pretty reliable guide to possibility, right?

EVA: Sure. Go on.

GENE: Okay. Well, I can imagine it turning out that God exists. I might have to wait until I die for confirmation, but His existing is at least imaginable. By the same token, I can imagine it turning out that there's no God. So, if imagination indicates possibility, God's existence and His nonexistence should both be possible. But as you say, that can't be if God is a necessary existent. What's gone wrong?

EVA: Well, there are two points, really. First, when you insist that God's existence is *possible*, you might just mean that *it could turn out* that God exists—that we don't *know for sure* that He doesn't exist.

GENE: Right.

EVA: Okay, but that's not the relevant notion of possibility. For purposes of the ontological argument, the term "possible" doesn't mean "as far as I know." After all, I *do* know I exist—it's *not* true that for all I know I don't exist. Even so, I might not have existed—my nonexistence is possible. Right?

GENE: Right, I see. So the possibility claims we've been debating aren't claims about knowledge or what we might discover to be true. They're about how the world *might have been*—possible worlds.

EVA: Exactly. That's that sort of possibility that imagination is supposed to establish. Also, there's imagination in a loose sense, and then there's *imagination*.

THEO: Oh, here we go.

EVA: Imagination can be a good guide to possibility, but we have to be careful. You've got to imagine something clearly and completely. Otherwise, all bets are off. And the more complicated the scenario, the harder it is to be sure that you're imagining it clearly and completely. Have you guys heard of Goldbach's conjecture?

THEO: Gold-who?

GENE: Yeah, I know it. "Any even integer greater than two can be expressed as the sum of two primes."

EVA: Right. As of today, the conjecture is unproved. No one knows for sure if it's true or false. Now, can you imagine that's true?

GENE: Um, I suppose so.

EVA: And can you imagine it's false?

GENE: Sure, I guess.

EVA: But of course *if* it's true, then it's necessarily true. And if it's false then it's necessarily false. All mathematical truths are necessary in that way. No matter how the world might have been, 2 + 2 = 4. And, no matter how the world might have been, 2 + 2 doesn't equal 5.

THEO: So this is like the God case. When we're talking possible worlds, Goldbach's conjecture is an all-or-nothing affair.

EVA: Right. And also like the God case, the underlying issues are complicated. So, it's unlikely that imagination is going to get you very far in determining whether or not it's really possible. The mere fact that you understand what Goldbach's conjecture says doesn't mean you're clearly and completely imagining its possibility. Likewise, just because you understand what it means to talk about God doesn't show that you're clearly and completely imagining His possibility either.

GENE: Ah, so that casts doubt on the first premise of the improved ontological argument. Maybe we can imagine God existing. But can we imagine that clearly and completely? I'm not too sure.

EVA: Right, assuming "imagination" means clear and complete imagination. If it doesn't mean that, the first premise may be fine. But then the second premise, which connects imaginability and possibility, is doubtful.

THEO: Of course, these considerations create the same problems for the ontological argument *against* the existence of God, right?

EVA: Maybe, but actually this isn't so clear. I find it pretty easy to imagine various scenarios that are incompatible with God's existence. I think I can imagine them about as clearly and as completely as you please—a possible world where everyone in it lives in excruciating pain, for example.

GENE: Speaking of which, have either of you got an aspirin?

THEO: Nope.

EVA: See, there is no God.

THEO: Not so fast. Gene clearly deserves what he gets.

GENE: Hey!

EVA: Gene, with a little aspirin, you think you could make the Art Institute?

GENE: I think so.

EVA: Okay. Enough imagining. Let's go see the possible worlds painted by the masters.

THEO: I think I'll get some aspirin as well. If we keep having these conversations, I'm going to need it.

6

Somewhere in Iowa

Religious Experience, Testimony, and Miracles

GENE: Wow, this is flat.

THEO: Get used to it. We're west of the Mississippi now. We're not going to see so much as a hill until we hit the Rockies.

EVA: And the corn. I never knew the world had so much corn. It just goes on and on.

THEO: America's Breadbasket, they call it. Part of the waves of amber grain with which God blessed America.

EVA: Oh, give me a break.

THEO: Ha ha. I just said that to annoy you.

EVA: Mission accomplished.

GENE: Aw, I was all excited about hearing a new argument about the existence of God. The argument from Iowa. The Iowalogical argument!

EVA: I'm not sure which way that argument points.

GENE: Hey now. My dad was born in this fine state. I'll hear nothing bad about it.

THEO: That's right, I forgot about that. Are your grandparents still here?

GENE: They are. And they'll never leave.

EVA: Ouch, that's a grim way of putting it.

GENE: They're dead. They've been dead for years.

THEO: That's what I love about you, Gene: your sentimentality. Where did they live?

GENE: Not far from here, actually. Around Dyersville.

THEO: Dyersville, Dyersville…. How do I know that name?

GENE: It's the setting for that old baseball movie, *Field of Dreams*.

THEO: Ah, right. "If you build it, they will come." Right?

GENE: That's the one. With Kevin Costner.

EVA: I think I've heard of that. What's this "build it and they will come" stuff?

THEO: Kevin Costner is tooling around in a field in Dyersville, and the spirit of this old baseball player…

GENE: Shoeless Joe.

THEO: Shoeless Joe comes out of the corn and tells Costner to build a baseball field.

GENE: And Costner points out that no one's going to come to the middle of Iowa just to watch baseball. Shoeless Joe says, ominously, "If you build it, they will come."

EVA: So let me guess. He builds it, and they come. End of movie.

THEO: Pretty much.

EVA: Man, it's a good thing Shoeless Joe didn't tell him to build a Gulag.

GENE: No kidding.

EVA: People in the 80's must have been pretty gullible.

THEO: It was a pretty good movie, actually. One of the best baseball movies of all time.

EVA: I'm not sure that tells me much.

THEO: You just don't like baseball.

EVA: Or football, or basketball, or hockey…

THEO: But if you liked sports, you might get into it.

EVA: I think I'd have a hard time swallowing the bit about the ghost coming out of the corn.

THEO: Aw, c'mon. It's a movie. And how do you know there are no ghosts? As far as you know, a ghost could come out of the cornfield at any moment.

GENE: Well if it did, I sure as hell wouldn't be sticking around to build any baseball diamonds.

EVA: Me neither.

THEO: So you admit there could be ghosts?

EVA: I admit no such thing.

GENE: Oh, c'mon Eva. You can imagine seeing a ghost, can't you? Even if you haven't seen this movie, you've seen others with ghosts. So you can imagine it. And if you can imagine it, it's possible.

EVA: This is a perfect example of what we were talking about yesterday. Imagining something shows it's possible only if you clearly and completely imagine it. The fact that I can create a mental picture of a slightly translucent being talking to me doesn't show anything about the possibility of ghosts. At best it shows the possibility of holograms or projections of light.

GENE: But Shoeless Joe wasn't translucent.

EVA: Even so, when you begin to imagine these things in detail, it's doubtful that they're coherent. In some of these movies, the ghosts do things like toss baseballs and also walk through walls. But you've got to be solid to throw a baseball. And if you're solid, you can't walk through walls.

THEO: Maybe those ghosts solidify when they want to. Or maybe non-solid things *can* throw baseballs.

EVA: I doubt it, but the point is that until your imagination is so clear as to allow all these things to be worked out, you can't be confident you're imagining a real possibility.

GENE: That stuff happens only in the movies anyway. Let's forget about it.

THEO: I'm not sure it happens only in the movies.

EVA: And I'm not sure we should forget about it. I think it might be relevant to our debate about God.

GENE: All roads lead back there, huh? Eva, you're obsessed.

THEO: Actually, I agree with her. All the arguments we've discussed so far are based on arcane philosophical principles. It's as though we're assuming you have to *reason* your way to belief in God. But that's not the path most people take to belief.

EVA: You're right. Most people just follow like sheep.

THEO: I don't think that's true. I'll bet most people believe because they've had religious experiences—experiences of perceiving God's presence. Either that or they rely on the testimony of others who have had such experiences.

GENE: Experiences? What do you mean, visions?

THEO: Maybe visions. Maybe hearing the voice of God. Or maybe seeing miracles performed in God's name.

GENE: And you've had such experiences?

THEO: No, but I accept the word of people who have.

EVA: You know such people?

THEO: I didn't say I know them. Not like I know you, anyway. I have their testimony. In the Bible, for instance.

GENE: Oh no, not that old argument!

THEO: Which argument?

GENE: God exists because the Bible says so.

THEO: Well, that's one way of putting it. Why not?

GENE: Why believe the Bible?

EVA: Because it's the word of God.

GENE: Exactly! You believe that God exists because the Bible says He does. And you believe what the Bible says because ... it's the word of God! That's circular reasoning. It's like trusting a fortuneteller because she says that she sees in her crystal ball that all of her fortunes will come true.

THEO: Hold on now. I didn't say I believed the Bible because it was the word of God. Eva said that.

GENE: Okay, so you believe in God because the Bible teaches that God exists. Why believe in the Bible? What evidence do you have for the claim that the Bible is a reliable source?

THEO: Well, the fact that so many people believe it is one reason.

EVA: How could that be a reason? Once lots of people believed the Earth was flat, but it's not. There are all sorts of reasons why so many people believe in God, not least because historically many of the people who didn't died by the sword!

GENE: Not to mention the fact that most people don't believe the Bible. Jews don't believe the New Testament. Muslims don't believe a lot of it. And Hindus, Buddhists, and atheists believe almost none of it. In fact, those who don't believe it outnumber those who do by quite a bit. Worldwide, it's about two to one.

THEO: If you put it that way, you're right, it doesn't sound reasonable. But listen: why do you believe anything you read or hear about? Suppose you buy a book on the history of China. Why believe what it says? You've never been there. Maybe you don't even know anyone who has.

GENE: Maybe you believe it because the author's an expert on China.

THEO: And how do you know she's an expert?

GENE: Because it says so on the back of the book. Maybe it says she has a PhD from Harvard, that she's a professor at a respectable university, and that she studied in China. Things like that.

EVA: And there may be quotes from other known experts on the back of the book, praising it for being well researched.

THEO: So you're saying you trust the book because the book tells you to? Because it says that the author is an expert and the book is well researched? How is that any better than my reasoning about the Bible?

GENE: That's a clever way of turning the tables on us, Theo. But there's a difference here.

EVA: There's definitely a difference.

THEO: I'd like to hear it.

EVA: Just give me a second.

THEO: And don't tell me you can't know anything about China in this way. If I'm as reasonable in believing in God as most people are in believing in the Qing Dynasty, I'll be happy.

GENE: She said to wait a second!

The three remain silent as the car continues to pass through the Iowa corn. After a few minutes, Theo turns on the radio and flips it to a station on which a sermon is being aired. Theo grins and turns it up.

RADIO: And the angel said unto her, Fear not, Mary: for thou hast found favour with God…

EVA: Okay, Theo. A joke's a joke. Turn it off.

GENE: No, hold on a second.

RADIO: And in the fourth watch of the night Jesus went unto them, walking on the sea...

GENE: I've got it!

Theo turns off the radio.

THEO: Okay, let's hear it.

GENE: Well, among other things, the book about China and the Bible are testifying to very different things.

THEO: I should hope so.

GENE: Suppose the book on Chinese history not only said that the Qing Dynasty lost land to the Mongols, but also that the Qing emperors used ghost soldiers when battling Genghis Khan. I take it that the endorsement of even the best experts wouldn't bring you to believe that.

THEO: No, probably not.

GENE: In fact, it would probably lead you to doubt the book's other claims. Right?

THEO: Right. I'd at least want to check them against another source.

GENE: So when we hear that Jesus walked on water and rose from the dead, or that Moses parted the Red Sea, shouldn't the same reasoning apply? It's one thing to take someone's word for something. It's quite another to believe anything someone says.

EVA: So now the tables are turned back on you, Theo. Why be skeptical about the Chinese history book that talks about ghost soldiers and not about the Bible that talks about wrestling angels?

GENE: Feel free to take a few minutes.

THEO: Well, for one thing, in the Bible there are multiple sources of testimony for the miracles of Jesus. The Bible wasn't written by just one person. Many people contributed.

GENE: Yeah, but in many cases the different accounts conflict. And in any case, it's not as though these sources were completely independent. Take the Gospels, for example. Mark wrote his gospel first, and there's evidence that Matthew and Luke used it as a source. So it's hard to know what they got from Mark and what they didn't.

THEO: That's true. But historians have been scrutinizing the Bible for a long time. Scholars have, in effect, vetted it.

EVA: I'm not sure that's a good thing. I'd wonder what's been changed over the years.

GENE: Right. Maybe the book on China is published and then goes through several editions passed on by scanner or computer disk. But compare the New Testament. It wasn't scanned. It was copied by scribes with varying skills and diverse motives. It's well known that many changes were made by scribes over the centuries, sometimes intentionally. For example, the famous scene at the end of Matthew when Jesus appears to the disciples after his resurrection: that's an addition that wasn't in the original.

EVA: Wow. How do you know all this?

GENE: I heard a talk by a scholar named Bart D. Ehrman. One of his more memorable lines was that there are as many different versions of the New Testament as there are words in the book.

THEO: I'd have to see his evidence for that.

EVA: Good! You *should* look for evidence that Ehrman is a reliable scholar! I wouldn't have you rely on a source without knowing how he got the knowledge he has, and without your having an independent reason for believing he's a good source.

GENE: But if you hold Ehrman to that standard, you should hold your Bible to that same standard, Theo.

THEO: Wait a second. You're comparing the work of this guy Ehrman to the Bible? Give me a break.

GENE: I'm only saying that if you hold one source to a standard, you should hold all sources to that standard. If you think you have to subject Ehrman's findings to scrutiny before forming a responsible belief based on what he says, you should take the same attitude toward the Bible.

EVA: And remember, you can't excuse the Bible from this scrutiny by saying it's the word of God, because God's existence is what's at issue. That would get you back to the circular reasoning you wanted to avoid.

THEO: Granted. Still, there are some texts that could reasonably be taken as basic. The Bible is one such text. Some recent book by a scholar isn't.

EVA: How about the Qur'an? Or the Hadith?

GENE: Or the Upanishads or The Book of Mormon?

EVA: Or the many books recording the teachings of the Buddha? All of these books claim divine origin. And all say things that conflict with claims made in the Bible.

THEO: Well, I don't know much about those books.

EVA: Of course you don't. But many worshipers of other faiths don't know much about your book either. With the exception of The Book of Mormon, all of them imply that Jesus isn't divine. The Qur'an expressly maintains that he was a prophet, just as Abraham and Mohammad were, but that he was no son of God, born of a virgin.

GENE: And though the Mormons accept the divinity of Jesus, they believe in a number of revelations you don't believe.

THEO: So what's your point? I choose to believe the Bible. Everyone else can believe what they want.

GENE: Let's back up for a second. You said the Bible can be treated as a basic text. If the Bible asserts some proposition, then you should accept that proposition as true—even if it can't be independently verified. The Bible has that special status because it's divinely inspired.

THEO: Right.

GENE: Okay, then why believe that the Bible is divinely inspired and that the other books we mentioned aren't?

THEO: Well, I was practically born reading the Bible.

GENE: Does that make it more likely to be accurate? Or divinely inspired?

EVA: Let's think about a parallel case. Say you ask four friends to tell you the dates of the Qing Dynasty. Each one goes and checks a different website. Each site claims to be authoritative and to be read and relied upon by millions. When your friends return, each has a different answer. What should you do? Randomly choose one of the four answers? Or withhold belief until you investigate further to determine which site is reliable?

THEO: Withhold belief, obviously.

GENE: What if one of the sites is your home page? And what if the programmers who made your browser set that site as your home page?

EVA: Yeah, and let's suppose other, equally good browsers have the other sites as home pages.

THEO: Unless I had reason to believe the people who set my home page had special access to the truth, I would still withhold belief.

EVA: Right! Its being your home page doesn't make it any more likely to be right, especially given that others have home pages that say different things. Given this conflict, you have to delve further. You shouldn't be confident your home page is reliable. And you shouldn't regard your home page as a basic text—even if it was set as your home page by the programmers who made your browser.

THEO: So, you're saying that even though I grew up with the Bible as my, so to speak, home page, I shouldn't treat it as a basic text. I can't be confident that it's a reliable source of information. And that's because I know other people have other sacred texts—other home pages—with the same credentials, but which contradict the Bible.

GENE: That's right.

THEO: Well, I admit it's an interesting analogy. But your reasoning has a problem.

GENE: What's that?

THEO: In this case, all of the texts competing with the Bible are religious. Even though most aren't Christian, they're all religious. They all endorse the existence of God—or of some supreme deity anyway. That's all I was trying to prove.

GENE: So you're giving up on the rationality of Christianity?

THEO: I didn't say that! I'm just saying that even if I accept your argument, I can still conclude that God exists, based on the consensus of basic texts.

EVA: It's no surprise that all the basic texts say God exists.

THEO: Why?

EVA: Because, you bonehead, we've been calling texts "basic" only if they claim divine inspiration! It would be a surprising text that claimed to be inspired by God but then denied there was such a thing!

THEO: True.

EVA: And if we expand "basic texts" to mean texts that people just happen to treat as authoritative, then there'd be no consensus on the existence of God. I'm inclined to take Lucretius' *De Rerum Natura* as my basic text, and it explicitly denies there's a god. Someone else might be inclined to take the works of David Hume as basic. Those works also deny there's a god. Well, sort of.

GENE: Sort of? What, was Hume agnostic?

EVA: No, but his most famous work on religion was written in dialogue form, so you have to extrapolate a little from what the characters say. But the atheistic message comes across pretty clearly, to me at least. It's no accident that he didn't publish the dialogue until after he died.

GENE: Philosophers don't still write in dialogue form, do they? It seems like such a cop-out—a way to avoid having to take a stand. Just have the characters disagree!

Theo clears his throat loudly.

GENE: Sorry, that was a tangent I guess.

THEO: Look, Eva, the books you mention are irrelevant. No one takes them as basic in the same way that Christians take the Bible as basic. You don't take Lucretius on faith.

EVA: I guess that's true. Taking something on faith is more or less equivalent to treating it as the word of God or a spirit or something. I doubt many would take anything on faith unless they thought it had a supernatural origin. I suspect it happens occasionally, though.

GENE: It definitely happens, Eva. Speaking of China, for instance, there were certainly times when quoting Mao or Confucius was considered the end of the matter.

EVA: Okay, but did the people you're talking about think of Mao or Confucius as merely human, or as somehow divine?

GENE: Maybe they did think of them as somehow divine. In addition, though, not all of the so-called basic texts endorse a god of the sort the Abrahamic religions believe in. For example, the Hindu notion of divinity is quite different, and many Buddhists don't believe in anything like a transcendent deity.

THEO: Well, this may sound crass, but if those texts don't talk about a perfect God, then so much the worse for them. God's perfection is so central to my belief that any text that doesn't embrace it isn't even a candidate for a basic text for me.

EVA: Aha! Theo's dogmatism finally shows its face.

GENE: Hold on, Eva. Don't be so quick to judge. Let's hear your side of it, Theo.

THEO: I think I've been clear about my views.

GENE: Not entirely. You've provided no reason to believe the Bible is more reliable than any number of sources that contradict it on your main contention that a perfect God exists. You haven't even tried to show that. So why are you so confident in what the Bible says about God?

THEO: I think it comes down to something I sense. I'll explain, but first I want to say something more about evidence. I just remembered something. There's evidence for God's existence that even Eva will have a hard time rejecting.

GENE: This I've got to hear.

THEO: It concerns her heroes.

GENE: You mean Jan-Ove Waldner, the old Swedish table tennis star?

THEO: I said *her* heroes, not yours, you nerd. I mean leading philosophers.

EVA: If you're talking about Descartes and Leibniz, I'm not impressed. I know they were theists, as were so many historical figures. Great thinkers, but I think their brains got mushy when it came to the divine. And they were of their time, so to speak.

THEO: I'm not talking about those guys. I'm talking about the leaders in your field: top philosophers such as Hilary Putnam, Saul Kripke, and Peter van Inwagen. I've read that they believe in God just like I do.

EVA: Huh.

GENE: So what?

THEO: If experts endorse a proposition in their area of expertise, that itself is evidence of its truth—evidence nonexperts should take seriously. Those philosophers must have thought a lot about the issues we've been discussing. And they've concluded that God exists.

EVA: I don't know about that argument. First of all, if you're going to appeal to expert philosophical opinion, you should look at the whole field. As a matter of fact, only about 15% of philosophers believe.

GENE: Really? So few!

EVA: Yep. Far fewer than in the general population. But I'm not sure it matters if philosophers believe. It depends on why they believe. I doubt most theist philosophers believe on the basis of the evidence. And if their theism isn't based on a rational assessment of the evidence, then their expertise is irrelevant.

GENE: Why?

Eva: Because then they're just believing because of faith or something like that. And the fact that others have faith doesn't provide any evidence that God exists—even if those others are top philosophers. Of course, they might believe for rational reasons. But in that case, let's hear their arguments.

Theo: Some reasons for belief aren't easily expressed as straightforward arguments in the sense that, for example, Paley's reasons or Anselm's reasons are.

Gene: I wouldn't call Anselm's argument easy or straightforward.

Theo: Anyway, as I was saying before, ultimately I believe in God because it's something I sense. It's something that I perceive about the world.

Eva: Hold on now. You haven't been talking to any burning bushes, have you?

Theo: No, my own experiences haven't been that radical, though I don't doubt that such things happen. Religious experiences come in many varieties, as your buddy William James would say. Not all of them are of the sort that involves visions.

Eva: What in the world are you talking about?

Theo: If you don't believe, or if you're so wedded to explicit proof and reasoning so that you can't count anything else as a reason to believe—well, then I doubt you'd understand.

Gene: Try us.

Eva grumbles.

Gene: Try me, anyway.

Theo: I won't go into details. If you want those, you can't do any better than reading James. He discusses a wide variety of religious experiences. The central feature is the sense that you're not alone—that you're loved and protected by an immensely powerful and infinitely caring being. Paradoxically, though, at the same time that there's this sense of being loved and valued, you also have the sense that your own concerns and distractions are trivial in comparison to the greatness of this force. And when I say it's a force, I mean it seems just as present as the two of you here in this car, if not more so.

Eva: Does it seem that way now?

Theo: Well, no. I know that God is with all of us now and all the time, but it's not as though at every moment I'm directly perceiving His presence. That happens less frequently, and it's not really something you can force. I guess the best comparison is with being in love. There are times when the feeling is simply too much to bear, and then there are times when it's more in the background, warming you but not searing your consciousness.

GENE: That sounds pretty good.

THEO: You've never had that experience?

GENE: No, not really.

EVA: Definitely not.

THEO: I can't even imagine my life without it. That's why I can't even begin to entertain a worldview that doesn't involve a benevolent all-powerful God.

EVA: Even though I can't really relate, I do think you're onto something. The history of religion is filled with individuals who have conversion experiences. Very rarely do you hear of anyone converting because of an argument.

THEO: Absolutely. That's one reason I haven't been too concerned that you've picked holes in the arguments we discussed earlier. At most, those arguments buttress my belief. They don't form its foundation. My experiences do.

GENE: That's pretty compelling stuff.

THEO: It is to me.

GENE: But I guess it's just bad luck for those of us who don't have those experiences. I don't doubt that you have them. But just knowing you do isn't enough for me.

THEO: I understand. I wouldn't believe just because someone else told me about such an experience.

EVA: I think that reasoning is pretty suspicious.

GENE: What's wrong with it?

EVA: You guys remember that little road running alongside the interstate for a few miles back?

GENE: No, I was paying attention to Theo.

THEO: I do.

EVA: Well, did you see that green tractor turning onto that road from a gravel driveway?

THEO: No, I didn't see that.

GENE: Nor did I.

EVA: Well, I did see it. I was looking out the window while Theo was speaking.

GENE: So what was so unusual about this tractor?

EVA: Absolutely nothing.

THEO: That's a really good story, Eva. So exciting. You should turn it into a screenplay.

EVA: But you both believe there was a tractor, right?

THEO: Unless you're just playing with us. Are you playing with us?

EVA: No, I'm serious. There was a tractor.

GENE: Sure, I believe it.

THEO: Sure.

EVA: See! That's interesting.

GENE: I don't get it.

EVA: What's interesting is that you both believe that there was a tractor there simply because I sincerely told you I perceived it. When Theo tells us, quite sincerely, that he perceives a higher force, we believe he had an experience, but we don't simply take his word for it that there really is a higher force.

GENE: That's true.

EVA: Well, I can think of only a few reasons why that might be. Maybe we don't believe he had the experience he says he had. He might be making it up. Or maybe he's just misremembering or misdescribing it.

GENE: No, I'm willing to take his word that his experience is as he says it was.

EVA: I am too. So that leaves only one other possibility: we believe having an experience like that isn't good evidence for the existence of a God. But when I tell you I perceived a tractor, not only do you believe I had a certain visual experience, but you form the belief that there was a tractor. So, you think the fact that someone had that experience is good evidence for the presence of a tractor.

GENE: Sounds right.

EVA: So, my question for both of you is this. You say that someone else's having the religious experience doesn't lead you to believe, but not because you doubt they had that experience. Then why would *your* having the experience make any difference? All that tells you is what you already knew—that there are such experiences. What you questioned, apparently, was whether the having of such experiences indicated the existence of God. But that's a question about the connection between the experience and God. You don't learn anything more about that connection by having the experience yourself.

THEO: I get it. You're saying that if I think religious experiences are good evidence for the existence of God, then it shouldn't matter whether I'm not one who's having them. That anyone has such experiences would be good evidence for me.

EVA: Exactly.

THEO: Okay, I buy that. I started out by saying that the experiences of others as documented in the Bible provide evidence for me. So I'm with you.

GENE: But didn't you say that if you hadn't had these experiences you probably wouldn't believe?

THEO: Yeah, I said that, and maybe I wouldn't believe. That doesn't mean I shouldn't.

GENE: I don't know. Even though I believe you're feeling all the things you claim to be feeling, that simply doesn't do it for me. So I guess by Eva's argument, I should be suspicious of the evidence of such experiences even if one day I have them too.

EVA: I think it ultimately comes down to this: even though we know religious experiences can be very compelling, we should still be suspicious of them. It's somewhat unlike perception in that way.

THEO: I never said my religious experiences were exactly like perceptions. Having a religious experience isn't just like seeing or hearing. It's something else.

EVA: I understand you don't think you're literally seeing with your eyes or touching with your fingers. But that's part of the problem.

THEO: Why is that a problem? It could be that there are other ways of perceiving—spiritual ways.

EVA: You can say that, but there's an important difference.

THEO: How so?

EVA: Well, do you think religious experiences are infallible?

THEO: What do you mean?

EVA: Do you think they ever mislead? I mean, there can be visual and auditory hallucinations or misperceptions. Can religious experiences go awry in the same way?

THEO: I don't know. I don't think mine do.

GENE: Eva's not talking about yours. She's asking whether there might be cases when someone seems to be having a genuine religious experience, but in fact she's not—her experience is inaccurate in the way that hallucination or misperception is inaccurate. If religious experience is like perception, that should be possible, since it happens with the rest of our senses.

THEO: Yeah, I suppose so. There can be inaccurate religious experiences. If I denied that, then I'd have to say that everyone who sincerely claims to be having a revelation really is having one. But many so-called revelations indicate a far different god than the one I believe in.

GENE: No doubt.

EVA: Okay, so how do we know I wasn't hallucinating that tractor back there?

THEO: Come to think of it, we don't!

EVA: Oh, come on.

GENE: Well, for one thing we can go back there and check.

EVA: Right.

GENE: We can check your other visual reports to see if what you see really is there.

EVA: And if I'm alone, I can always reach out my hand and try to touch what I see. If I can't confirm what one sense tells me by using another sense, I know something's probably wrong.

THEO: And if we had the equipment we could check your eyes and the visual processing centers of your brain to see if there's something going on that might cause you to have visions.

EVA: That's right, we could do all those things, at least in principle. Now, what can be done to tell whether your religious experiences are accurate?

THEO: You mean, granting that I'm having the experiences I say I'm having, how can you tell whether they're actually detecting a divine presence?

EVA: Not only how can *we* tell, but how can *you* tell?

GENE: Well, one thing's for sure, we can't just go and check as we can with the tractor. Because the rest of us can sit where you're sitting but feel nothing.

EVA: And you can't confirm what you sense by using your other senses, such as sight and touch, can you?

THEO: No.

GENE: And since there's no organ dedicated to religious perception, in the way eyes and the certain parts of the brain are dedicated to sight, we can't check to make sure that organ's working properly.

THEO: Well, you could check to see if my brain's functioning well generally.

GENE: True, but that wouldn't be enough to determine accuracy.

EVA: So, unlike seeing, hearing, and the like, there's no way to gage the accuracy of your experiences.

THEO: Okay, all of what you say may be true. But God can do anything. He can touch my mind directly. We shouldn't expect him to make noise for my ears or reflect light into my eyes. We should expect religious experience to work differently—to be more private, for example.

EVA: I don't disagree. But that doesn't solve the problem. You admit there are people who believe they're having religious experiences but aren't actually in touch with God. Without any way of judging the accuracy of such experiences, you have no basis for claiming that yours are authentic and theirs aren't.

THEO: Maybe so. Nevertheless, I can't shake the sense that, when I have these experiences, I'm perceiving a divine, loving presence. It just seems overwhelmingly clear.

GENE: But others probably feel similarly—others whose experiences indicate to them a very different sort of god than the one you're sure you sense.

THEO: I guess I have to live with that. Now, if you can agree to live with that too, I say we play some tunes.

EVA: As long as it's not The Eagles. Or Dave Matthews.

GENE: I have just one more question about these experiences.

THEO: Ah, Gene, now you're not going to let me off the hook?

GENE: I'm not really against you here, Theo. I'm still pretty sure that if I had such experiences I'd be in your shoes—whether or not that's rational. I'm just genuinely interested.

THEO: Okay, then, shoot.

GENE: Doesn't it trouble you that there might be quite natural, scientific explanations for the religious experiences you're talking about?

THEO: What do you have in mind?

GENE: In some of the more extreme cases, I've heard that they've found brain damage—lesions, tumors, or signs of schizophrenia.

THEO: It's not impossible that God chooses brain damage as a channel for His communication.

GENE: True. But one wonders why an all-powerful God would express himself through brain lesions.

THEO: Well, I admit brain damage might explain some of the wackier experiences, but not the sort that I have. At least I hope not.

GENE: I'm sure your brain's doing fine. But there are other, less physiological factors that might explain your experiences.

THEO: There are indeed.

GENE: No, I'm not referring to God's presence. There are sociological explanations of religious experiences. There are also psychological explanations.

THEO: Great. So you think there's either something wrong with my brain or I'm a lunatic?

GENE: No, hear me out. People who are depressed often don't think of themselves as having a mood disorder. Instead, they feel as though they perceive a lack of value in the world. They tend to say things like, "Of course I'm sad. The world stinks and life has no meaning." To someone who's clinically depressed, such "insights" can be irresistible and come with real conviction. How can you be sure that your feeling isn't like that, only in reverse?

THEO: Why would I think it is?

GENE: There's a pattern for these things. People often become born again when they're adolescents and feel out of place. Sometimes these teenagers are taken under the wing of a believer. Those people often report the sorts of experiences you report, as do people who have reached rock bottom in their lives and feel their only option is to turn to a higher power.

THEO: Neither of those cases describes me, but in any case this doesn't sound very scientific. It sounds like a bunch of generalizations after the fact. Would you be willing to maintain that anyone put in these circumstances would act similarly?

GENE: No. Human beings are complicated creatures, and I don't pretend to know all the factors involved.

THEO: Plus, who are you to say that people in such circumstances aren't just more likely to find God? Maybe God has special reasons for making contact then.

GENE: I suppose. But again, it seems suspicious.

THEO: I don't see why.

EVA: Oh, come on, Theo. In the situations Gene is talking about, people are more likely to be pulled into cults of all kinds. It's when they're at their most fragile, psychologically. Doesn't that cast doubt on the reliability of their religious experiences?

THEO: It might. But again, this all seems rather loose and speculative. I'd want to see the hard data. Also, you have to admit, none of your descriptions seem to fit my case, and there are many other people like me.

GENE: Fair enough.

EVA: But as psychology evolves…

THEO: It will probably evolve to explain why people like you are atheists. This sword cuts both ways.

GENE: Ooh. Nice shot, Theo.

EVA: Wait, something's amiss.

GENE: No, Eva, Theo's making a good point. We can't dismiss Theo's theistic reasoning just because psychology can explain it—any more than we can dismiss your atheistic reasoning on the same grounds.

EVA: No, there's a difference. Theo was trying to use his experiences as evidence for God's existence. I wasn't using my experiences as evidence for anything.

THEO: Okay, but my main point stands. The fact that psychology can explain my experiences without invoking God's existence doesn't automatically imply that my experiences don't count as evidence for God's existence.

Eva: True, but if there are reasonable nontheistic explanations of your experiences, then why should anyone—including you—accept the theistic explanation?

Theo: Why shouldn't I?

Eva: Because there are better explanations. Hume nailed this point, in his discussion of miracles.

Gene: Oh no, not another argument from Hume's authority! Were you actually serious when you suggested that his corpus is your version of Holy Scripture?

Eva: Oh, please. I'm just trying to give credit where credit is due. Here's the sort of point I have in mind:

> When anyone tells me, that he saw a dead man restored to life, I immediately consider with myself, whether it be more probable, that this person should either deceive or be deceived, or that the fact, which he relates, should really have happened. I weigh the one miracle against the other; and according to the superiority, which I discover, I pronounce my decision, and always reject the greater miracle. If the falsehood of his testimony would be more miraculous, than the event which he relates; then, and not till then, can he pretend to command my belief or opinion. (Hume)

Theo: Why are we all of a sudden talking about the dead returning from the grave?

Eva: That's just an example. The point is general. Suppose someone tells you that his great grandfather was dead for half a century but has been hanging around the dog track since last Thursday. Which is more likely? That grandpa came back to life? Or that his report is mistaken?

Theo: That the report is mistaken, of course.

Eva: Exactly. Why?

Theo: People often make mistakes. They exaggerate. They get stoned and imagine all kinds of wacky things. And they lie.

Eva: Right. Such things happen all the time. But what doesn't happen all the time is dead people coming back to life. That would be "the greater miracle," as Hume puts it. Therefore, the more reasonable conclusion is that the report is mistaken.

Theo: Are you saying I'm a stoner or a liar?

Eva: No. I'm just saying that Hume's point applies to how to explain your religious experiences. Which is more likely? The supernatural, theistic explanation that you prefer? Or a more mundane, naturalistic explanation that science could provide? Again, the answer is that the naturalistic explanation is more probable. Maybe we can't rule out the theistic explanation with complete certainty. But that's not saying much.

Theo: I think you're moving too quickly here...

Gene: Can we come back to this later on? All this corn we're passing is making me hungry.

Eva: Okay, I'll shut up now.

Theo: Thank God.

Eva: No, thank...

Theo and Gene: Ssshhh.

7
Holcomb, Kansas

The Problem of Evil

THEO: Well, here we are: Holcomb, Kansas. Not much to it, is there?

EVA: I don't think Disneyland has much to worry about.

GENE: I never promised Disneyland.

EVA: Yeah, but Gene! There's really nothing here!

GENE: It's smaller than I expected. And I guess I expected a sign or something. Did either of you see a sign?

THEO: The sign back there said Holcomb. It wasn't worth the trip, in my opinion.

GENE: No, I mean a sign about the Clutter murders or *In Cold Blood*.

THEO: It's a little creepy that you had us make this detour, Gene. I don't know how you convinced me.

EVA: Gene, did it ever occur to you that the people here probably don't want their town to be known for the murder of an innocent family? Did you think the city council promotes massacre tourism?

GENE: It's not massacre tourism: it's literary tourism! *In Cold Blood* is one of the best books in American letters, and this is where it's set. I don't have some macabre fascination with murder.

EVA: Okay, creep.

GENE: Oh, turn here, turn here! I think it's right down this lane that the Clutter family got it!

THEO: Man, you *are* creepy. It says no trespassing. I don't think we should…

GENE: Turn!

EVA: Better do what he says, Theo, or Holcomb might be the scene of another grisly crime.

THEO: Turning, turning…

GENE: That's it! That's the old Clutter Farm!

THEO: It's just a house.

GENE: Do you think they give tours?

THEO: No, I don't. Look, it's just a house. People are living there.

EVA: I don't know how you could live there after all that happened.

THEO: I thought you didn't believe in ghosts, Eva.

EVA: I don't. But that doesn't mean I don't get spooked in the middle of the night. And living in a house where a family was slaughtered…

THEO: I wouldn't want to live out here in the middle of nowhere, with no close neighbors or anything. If you screamed, no one would hear.

EVA: Okay, let's get out of here. Theo, let's go.

GENE: Wait just a second! Let me get a better picture. None of these…

EVA: Now!

THEO: Okay, okay. Sorry, Gene. It's spooky.

EVA: No kidding. The sooner we get back to civilization, the better.

GENE: I'm surprised at you, Eva. This isn't your normal, rational self. You know, you're almost certainly safer here than on the interstate.

THEO: Or in the middle of New York City, where you keep saying you're going to live.

EVA: I don't know. New York has so many people, even in the middle of the night you're near someone. You feel that if something happened, you could scream and hundreds of people would hear you. Out here…

THEO: You're assuming someone would help you if you screamed.

EVA: Now *you're* creeping me out, Theo.

GENE: No, Theo's right. Even in a crowded city bad things happen all the time and no one helps. Think of Kitty Genovese.

EVA: Kitty who?

GENE: Kitty Genovese. She was murdered near her apartment house in Queens, back in the 60's. People heard her screaming that she was being stabbed, but they didn't do anything about it. One guy yelled out of his window, and the attacker left for a bit, but he came back a little while later and finished the job.

EVA: Ech. Gene, where do you hear about this stuff?

GENE: The world is full of it. Ever watch the news?

EVA: Not for stuff like that. Besides, that happened way before you were born.

THEO: To be fair to Gene, I've heard of it too. It's pretty famous, actually. I heard about it in my psychology class. It's associated with what's called the bystander effect. People don't want to get involved.

GENE: That's exactly what one witness was quoted as saying. "I didn't want to get involved." At the time, some newspapers reported that one neighbor turned up his radio to drown out her screams.

EVA: That's disgusting. What sort of people are these?

THEO: Not good ones.

GENE: It's easy to say that, but would you have acted differently? Are you sure you'd have gotten involved?

THEO: I'd have at least called the police, and if I knew I wouldn't get seriously hurt I'd have directly intervened.

EVA: Did her neighbors even call the police?

GENE: Most of them didn't. Like I said, one of them is said to have turned up his radio…

EVA: That's just indecent.

THEO: Unforgivable.

GENE: You guys are pretty quick to condemn.

THEO: It's not exactly a hard call. These people could have prevented a murder without putting themselves in harm's way. That sort of indifference is immoral.

EVA: I agree.

GENE: I'd be careful about being so judgmental, Theo. According to you, there was another observer who didn't intervene on Kitty's behalf.

THEO: Oh, you've got to be kidding.

EVA: Gene's right! God was watching, and He certainly could have prevented the murder without harming himself or anyone else.

THEO: It's not God's job to jump in and prevent people from murdering.

EVA: Why? He doesn't want to get involved?

GENE: Sounds familiar.

THEO: It's not like that.

EVA: So what is it like?

THEO: You're telling me that you don't believe in God because Kitty Genovese got stabbed?

EVA: It's a pretty old argument, actually. People usually discuss the example of the Holocaust, not Kitty Genovese, but the point's the same.

THEO: You're referring to The Problem of Evil, right?

EVA: Right.

THEO: I knew this time would come. I'm surprised it took you so long. Let's hear it.

EVA: The argument can be stated concisely, if we let "evil" stand for things having negative moral value.

GENE: What does that mean?

EVA: The clearest examples are pain and suffering. Those things are morally bad. I mean: it's better if there's less of them, other things being equal.

GENE: So evil is pain or suffering?

EVA: Again, those are clear examples. But there might be other evils, such as the sort of loss that death can imply.

THEO: Hold on, Eva. "Evil" doesn't mean "pain, suffering, or death." Paper cuts cause pain but rarely involve evil.

EVA: Right, I know. I just need a term for negative moral value.

GENE: Hey, I just thought of one that's less misleading than "evil."

EVA: Do tell.

GENE: How about, "negative moral value"?

EVA: Cute. Look, I'll just use "evil." Sue me later if you want.

GENE: Won't be worth it. Philosophers aren't rich.

THEO: Okay, okay, enough. Eva, all you've done is redefined a word. Where's the argument you promised?

EVA: Here you go:

1. If God exists, there is no unnecessary evil.
2. There is unnecessary evil.
3. Therefore, God doesn't exist.

THEO: It's concise, I'll give you that much.

GENE: Yeah, but I suspect those short premises build in a lot of assumptions.

EVA: Not really. The main assumption is one we've agreed on: we're talking about God as He's traditionally conceived—all knowing, all powerful, and all good.

GENE: That fits Samuel Beckett's name for him, *omniomniomni*: omniscient, omnipotent, and omnibenevolent. But as we said before, not everyone thinks God is like that.

THEO: That conception is pretty central to the Judeo-Christian tradition, though. I wouldn't want to give it up.

GENE: Why not?

THEO: Well, first and foremost God must be worthy of worship. If He were a morally tainted character, He wouldn't be.

GENE: That's not so clear. The Greeks and Romans worshipped some shady characters. Zeus was an out-and-out philanderer among other things!

THEO: Yeah, and that's one of the reasons that the pagan religions are unappealing. Why would you worship a God like that?

EVA: Maybe because you thought that if you didn't you might get a lightning bolt through your forehead.

THEO: True, you might do it out of fear, but is that really worship? It sounds more like paying lip service to a tyrant.

EVA: What, fear can't inspire worship? C'mon! Fear and worship go together like peanut butter and jelly. Just ask a Catholic or a Jew.

THEO: That's not how I conceive of my relationship to God. I can hardly imagine choosing to make God a central part of my life, if I thought of things that way.

GENE: Okay, Theo, I see why you want God to be all good. But why all powerful?

THEO: He's supposed to have created everything! That takes a mighty powerful supreme being.

EVA: No kidding. I don't see why a universe creator would have to have zero limits on His power, but I see where you're coming from. But why think God has to know everything?

THEO: That's a little trickier, but part of the reason concerns His compassion. To be fully compassionate, He's got to truly understand everyone and everything; He can't be ignorant in any substantial way.

GENE: Okay, so much for motivating the omniomniomni conception. Let's get back to the problem of evil. Theo, how do you get around that argument? I'm guessing you agree with the second premise, that the world contains unnecessary evil.

THEO: Well… I'm not sure.

EVA: Oh, come on! Think of all of the Jews killed in the Holocaust, all of the children murdered and women raped in war and…well, like Gene said, just look at the news!

GENE: Now I see why people use the Holocaust example. But isn't the Kitty Genovese case enough to establish premise 2?

THEO: I don't think so. It's complicated. But I don't think I need to defeat premise 2 anyway. Premise 1 is false: God can coexist with unnecessary evil.

GENE: How's that? If God is all good, all knowing, and all powerful, then why would He allow the world to contain the suffering that it does?

THEO: Just look at your examples: the Holocaust, the Clutter murders, war crimes, Kitty Genovese. God didn't do those things. Those were human acts, human evils.

GENE: You're missing the point. The argument doesn't depend on God's performing any evil acts. The residents of Kew Gardens who heard Kitty Genovese screaming didn't stick the knife in her back. Their crime was failing to do anything to help her, despite hearing her cries for help. You thought that made them pretty bad. Why don't you hold God to the same standard?

THEO: You're forgetting about free will.

GENE: Go on.

THEO: God made us free. We can choose what we do. And by giving us free will, God gave us the ability to act morally and immorally. We don't always make the best choices. But without freedom, we'd be little more than automatons.

EVA: So you're saying we're to blame, not God? It's from our misuse of our God-given freedom that we get murders, the Holocaust, and other atrocities?

THEO: Right.

EVA: I'm not sure that gets God off the hook. It's not enough to say God gave us free will. You also have to say that it was worth it. Maybe it would have been better if we didn't have free will and there weren't so many evils.

THEO: Of course it was worth it! Granted, people commit unbelievably evil acts. The Holocaust was, well, a holocaust. Even so, the alternative is worse. Without free will, we'd just be a bunch of robots.

EVA: Maybe that'd be true if we had no free will at all, but that's not what I'm suggesting. Here's an analogy. Many nations, including ours, place a high premium on personal liberty. Perhaps they think that life without liberty is no better than death.

THEO: Sounds right to me.

EVA: Me too, I guess, but even nations who think this don't let their citizens do just anything. Citizens aren't allowed to murder each other. But they're still free for the most part. Giving up a little freedom is worth it to avoid the disasters of anarchy.

GENE: Right, so why wouldn't God give us free will and then just curb it occasionally?

THEO: How would that work?

GENE: Why not have Hitler die while cleaning his gun, before his murderous reign begins? God could just put a glitch in his memory, so he forgets the gun is loaded or something. Or maybe just change around his brain chemistry, so that he loses all his racism and hatred. Sure, that'd be an intervention, and it would compromise Hitler's free will. And maybe it'd take an option off the table for some misguided Germans. But would that have been so bad? Surely it would have been worth it. It's not as though intervening in that way would have made us unfree robots.

THEO: Maybe not, but where would it end? After stopping Hitler, He'd have to stop Stalin. And after Stalin, Mao. And Pol Pot. And so on and so on, until He'd have to stop the killing of Kitty Genovese. Then we're back to a world without free will.

EVA: That seems a little quick.

THEO: The point is, there's nowhere to draw the line. Or maybe He's already drawn it.

GENE: I doubt it. I agree that it's hard to know when to curtail liberties. That's a problem for governments as well. But you have to draw the line somewhere. If the line you draw allows the Holocaust, there's something wrong.

EVA: Besides, there seem to be ways that God could prevent human evils from occurring without restricting liberties or violating our free will. He could make it so that when Oswald aimed and shot at Kennedy, a wind blew the bullet off course. Oswald would still have freely pulled the trigger. He'd still have made an immoral choice for which he could be judged. It's just that his act wouldn't have had the same bad effect.

THEO: That's easy enough to imagine in isolation. But think about what it'd be like if God did that sort of thing all the time. You'd have bending knives and swerving bullets galore—a miracle for every bad decision. I don't think we'd be free in such a world.

EVA: Sure we would! Being free just means being able to *try* to do things. It doesn't mean always succeeding. Your actions needn't accomplish all you hope they would.

GENE: I think freedom might require more than that. In fact, I'm not even sure that genuine free will exists.

THEO: You don't believe in free will?

GENE: I'm pretty skeptical. But that's a topic for another occasion.

THEO: I don't see why you wouldn't believe in free will.

EVA: I think I know where he's coming from. But without getting into a completely different debate, maybe I can push the objection this way: Why couldn't God make us so that we just freely chose to do the right things?

THEO: So we're free and yet we always choose correctly? That doesn't add up. If God predetermines that we choose correctly, that we choose to do good things, then we can't do otherwise. We're not free.

EVA: Why doesn't God make it so that we *could* choose bad things but we just, in the end, don't? We always choose good things instead.

THEO: Because that's incoherent. Remember, earlier we agreed that God's being all-powerful doesn't mean He can do the impossible. He can't make round squares. Making us so that we're guaranteed to freely choose the good every time is impossible, like making a round square.

GENE: But if God's omniscient, He knows everything, right? That means He knows what decisions we'll make before we make them. Why doesn't that imply that we don't have free will?

THEO: That does seem odd, but I think He can know what we'll choose even if we do so freely. Someone's knowing what will happen doesn't have any direct implications about what determines what will happen. In particular, it doesn't imply that we won't cause ourselves to do what we will do.

GENE: Okay, I guess that's right. But if there's no impossibility there—if God can know that we'll do something even though we could have done otherwise—then why is it impossible to make us so that we always freely choose to act well?

THEO: Because if God sets things up so that we always act well, then we're not free to do otherwise—and so we're not truly free. Hey, do you guys know if we're going the right way? Is that the road to Denver?

EVA: I think so. Gene, if we get lost because of this detour…

GENE: Don't worry. We're destined to freely get to San Francisco. It's already written.

EVA: Yeah, I'm pretty sure we're going the right way. But listen. Even if you're right, and God can't make us so that we freely always choose the right actions, surely you admit there are ways we can influence each other significantly. What we do is heavily influenced, even if not completely determined, by the way we were raised, by those who teach us, and by our natural dispositions.

GENE: Actually, I'm inclined to think everything we do is completely determined by those things.

EVA: Maybe you're right, though I can see why Theo might want to resist that claim. Still, Theo, you've got to admit that what we do is at least strongly influenced by factors outside of our control—our environment, our genetics, etc.

THEO: Yes, but we can always buck the odds. Even someone brought up in a perfect home can choose to murder, and a child abandoned in the slums can wind up a saint.

GENE: That doesn't prove anything.

EVA: Hold on, Gene. Theo, even if you're right, surely you recognize that what we do is to some degree conditioned by our genetic and environmental inheritance.

THEO: Fair enough. I probably wouldn't have been making this drive if I hadn't inherited a car, for example.

GENE: Or if you hadn't met us.

EVA: And you agree that some crimes and murders are committed not because the murderers thought it a good idea to commit a crime and freely did so, but because they were crazy?

THEO: Maybe. I'm not sure.

GENE: Oh, come on! David Berkowitz, the Son of Sam, thought his dog was telling him to murder! Clearly that guy was nuts! Not only did he think his dog was talking to him; he actually did what he thought his dog told him to do!

EVA: You can't deny the existence of mental illness, Theo.

THEO: Of course not. Berkowitz and Manson were nuts. No question.

EVA: So would it have interfered with their free will to remove their mental illness? Wouldn't that actually have made them more free?

THEO: I don't know about that. But why focus on such lunatics?

EVA: Why not? All I need is one case. If God could have prevented the Son of Sam murders without interfering with anyone's free will—perhaps by making a world that didn't have mental illness—then He would have been wrong not to have done so. To put it another way, given that a perfect God would have done so, there must not be a perfect God.

GENE: Eva doesn't really need to point to cases like Son of Sam.

EVA: You're not about to trot out some other, more obscure mass murderer, are you?

GENE: No, I was just going to say that your point holds for normal people. You admit, don't you, Theo, that a parent, teacher, or leader can inspire people to act well without infringing on their free will?

THEO: Of course.

EVA: You'd better! On your view, Jesus' teachings made the world a better place, didn't they? Yet I don't think the Sermon on the Mount robbed anyone of their free will.

THEO: True.

EVA: So why not create better teachers?

GENE: Why not send down a Jesus every fifty years?

THEO: I can't believe what I'm hearing. God sends down His own son, the greatest teacher man has ever had, and you ask for more?

EVA: Sure, why not? I think if God existed He'd do something just like what Gene suggests. He wouldn't just send down His son and then let the world fight for two thousand years over whether or not he really was God's son! As great a teacher as Jesus was, it obviously wasn't enough. And if God existed, He'd have known that. That there aren't more teachers like Jesus despite the fact that the world obviously needs them is evidence that God doesn't exist.

THEO: What you're saying is absurd. It's not that Jesus wasn't enough or that his teachings weren't good enough. It's that people haven't listened. That's their choice.

GENE: But why haven't they listened?

THEO: I have no idea. Eva, why haven't you?

EVA: Ha ha. Very funny.

GENE: Seriously. God, knowing everything, knew we wouldn't listen. He also knew why: human psychology has limitations. We're often self-centered, we have limited memory capacity, and many of us aren't terribly compassionate.

THEO: Speak for yourself.

GENE: I am. I mean, I know that a child dies of hunger every five seconds, and that I can prevent some of those deaths if I give money to any one of many charities. Even though I know this, I buy books instead of checking them out of the library. I buy DVDs I don't need, and sometimes I only watch them once. And my collection of table tennis rackets is obscenely large.

THEO: So you're selfish. We knew that.

GENE: I don't think it's just me. Here we are, staying in hotels and ordering room service, while people are dying of hunger. People aren't hard-wired to keep these things in view. If God existed, wouldn't He have made sure we kept each other in mind a little more than we do?

THEO: Why are you blaming God for your shortcomings? I can't believe I'm even listening to this.

EVA: No, Theo, Gene's making a good point. We have certain capacities that have a lot to do with our tendency to do good and evil—our capacity to listen, remember, feel, and so on. The fact that we're made the way we are, so as to allow atrocities such as the mass killings in Rwanda to occur or to allow others to die of hunger while we remain in the lap of luxury. That indicates that those capacities weren't designed by a perfect God.

THEO: In other words, you're saying that God is partly responsible for the evils that humans commit, even if they chose of their own free will to perpetrate those evils? Because He didn't give them faculties that would have led to better decisions?

GENE: Precisely.

THEO: This sounds a bit like a rapist whining because his mother didn't cuddle him enough!

EVA: Lovely, Theo.

THEO: In any case, I don't see how you two can be so confident that humans are a flawed creation. If God made us so that our sentiments welled up so that we always did the right thing, we wouldn't have free will. He gave us room to make good or bad decisions. Bad decisions are bound to get made sometimes.

GENE: But evil acts aren't rare. They occur all the time.

THEO: What makes you so sure God hasn't struck just the right balance? Maybe we have enough free will to prove our moral worth and enough moral sense to know what to do if we chose to do it. Isn't the fact that there are a lot of saints as well as a lot of sinners an argument that He struck that balance?

GENE: I guess I can't rule that out. I don't know how to make the perfect man.

EVA: Or woman.

GENE: I have a clearer idea of that.

EVA: You're a pig. Fortunately, though, we don't have to resolve this free will business to show that God doesn't exist. Human beings don't cause all the unnecessary evil in the world. There's plenty of evil to go around, even without our handiwork.

THEO: Namely?

EVA: Well, think about unnecessary animal pain. There was a lot of that before humans even existed.

THEO: I don't know. Did dinosaurs feel pain as we know it?

EVA: Probably. But forget animal pain. Stick to humans. There's still plenty of unnecessary pain, suffering, and death that we didn't cause.

THEO: Such as?

EVA: I'll give you a hint: we're on our way to California.

GENE: Earthquakes!

EVA: Earthquakes, tsunamis, landslides, famines, floods, plagues … the list goes on. Hundreds of thousands died in the 2010 Haiti earthquake alone. I've been using murder as an example because that's what we were talking about. But the argument from evil could be run in terms of evil caused by natural disasters:

1. If God exists, there is no unnecessary evil caused by natural disasters.
2. There is unnecessary evil caused by natural disasters.
3. Therefore, God doesn't exist.

GENE: That's pretty compelling. Rejecting that reasoning would be like believing your house was designed by the perfect architect even though the roof leaks and the ceiling sags.

THEO: You'd still believe there was an architect, wouldn't you? You wouldn't believe the house just leapt from the ground.

EVA: That's just the argument from design again, Theo. We flogged that dead horse enough.

THEO: Who said it was dead? Anyway, I'm not convinced by your architecture analogy. What if it turns out that your roof doesn't just leak—it leaks into a cistern that provides drinking water for the house?

GENE: That'd be pretty neat.

THEO: Maybe that's what's happening here.

EVA: You might wonder why the leak and the cistern have to be in the middle of the living room, though.

THEO: Huh?

EVA: I'm just anticipating. You're planning to say that seemingly pointless evil serves some unknown purpose, right?

THEO: Exactly.

EVA: Well, that's probably so in some cases, but in all? Also, even if natural disasters always did some good, that wouldn't be enough. The purpose has to be worth the cost.

THEO: True.

EVA: Yeah, it's not hard to find silver linings in dark clouds. But if the darkness is worse than the silver or if the silver could have been gotten without the clouds, then the plan could be better than it is. We still have evidence against God's existence.

THEO: I don't think it's like that.

GENE: I don't know, Theo. I mean, I once heard a guy say that God gave us famines to curb population growth.

THEO: Yeah, I don't buy that.

GENE: Right. If God wanted to curb population growth, He wouldn't use a famine, would He? There are so many other methods that don't involve so much suffering. For example, he could have made us so that we became less fertile when we live in places where population growth would cause problems.

EVA: Why would God even care about population growth? He could just have the planet expand and become more fruitful every time a child is born!

THEO: Okay, so pointing out some good effects of bad things doesn't completely answer the argument from evil. Still, I think a case can be made that evil plays an important role in an overarching design.

EVA: Go for it.

THEO: Well, Eva, do you remember reading Heraclitus in our philosophy class?

EVA: "Everything is fire"? That Heraclitus?

THEO: That's the one, but that's not the part I had in mind. He also said opposites depend on one another. Light depends on darkness, odd depends on even, and so on. The same thing could be said about good and evil. You can't have one without the other. So, the suffering that exists is needed because without it the world wouldn't have goodness either.

EVA: I do remember that bit in Heraclitus.

THEO: So how about it?

EVA: If I remember correctly, the professor made a couple of distinctions when explaining what Heraclitus might have meant. Those might come into play here.

THEO: Okay.

EVA: You might mean good and evil couldn't exist without each other. Alternatively, your point might concern *knowledge* of good and evil. In that case you could allow that they could exist without each other. The point is rather that if we never encountered bad things we wouldn't understand good things. Moral knowledge requires contrast.

GENE: This is getting a bit abstract. Give me examples.

EVA: Sure. You know how a valley depends on a mountain? If you have a valley between two mountains, and you take away the mountains...

THEO: You get Kansas.

EVA: Basically. No more valley. A valley only exists in relation to the mountains that surround it. You couldn't have a world with only valleys and no mountains.

GENE: Right.

EVA: So, one idea is that good and evil are like that. There can't be a purely good world: one with only goodness and no badness. Likewise, there can't be a purely bad world.

GENE: What's the other idea?

EVA: That good and evil are related like wealth and poverty. In principle, everyone could be poor; alternatively, everyone could be rich.

GENE: Does that even make sense?

EVA: I don't see why not. Just imagine that the world didn't have limited resources. Or imagine a plague wiped out everyone except those in the highest tax bracket. They wouldn't stop being rich just because no one was poor anymore.

GENE: It might give new meaning to the phrase, "You can't find good help these days."

EVA: Ha ha. Still, there might be a different sort of dependence. If you've never experienced poverty, you won't appreciate wealth in the same way you would otherwise. And if no one were poor, maybe no one would think of themselves as wealthy.

GENE: In that case, the terms "rich" and "poor" might never be used, or even invented.

EVA: Right. But there'd still be people who are financially well off. So the point is that sometimes one thing doesn't depend on its opposite, though comprehending that thing might depend on being familiar with its opposite.

GENE: Got it. So which do you want to say holds for good and evil, Theo?

THEO: It's a lot more like the wealth case than the valley case. I don't want to say there can't be a world without any evil. That view might entail that heaven is impossible, and it's not.

GENE: Right, and it's not as though people fighting against evil had better be careful not to fight it too well or they'd wipe it out and poof, goodness would suddenly disappear!

EVA: And it's not as though if things start to get too good we had better keep someone around to torture just to make sure that goodness continues to exist.

THEO: Yeah, the role of evil in the world is to add the contrast that allows us to appreciate the good in the world. Evil adds pepper to the soup.

EVA: I'm sure that'd make the people dying in famines and floods feel great. "Don't fret, my suffering brethren: you're the pepper in the soup of my life!"

THEO: I wouldn't put it that way.

GENE: No, but Eva has a point. If the purpose of evil is to help people appreciate the good, then evil is distributed unfairly. Entire populations have inordinate amounts of suffering—constant pain, hunger and death—while a relatively small number of people have gold-plated toilet bowls and beach-front balconies. If the evil that exists were there to serve the purpose you're talking about, would this be the way things are?

EVA: Right. Wouldn't it be better for every person to have a certain amount of strife, but no one person have so much that it's unbearable for her?

THEO: I don't know. Maybe for some reason we need examples of people who live terribly painful lives.

EVA: I don't see why. But even if some examples are needed, why so many? And why are they so concentrated in specific areas like Africa and Bangladesh? And Europe and Russia during World War II? Why do people have it so good in places like the United States today?

THEO: I don't think the residents of New Orleans would see things that way, since Katrina.

EVA: Okay, but you get the point, don't you? Even if some suffering is needed, why so much? And surely it could be distributed more justly. Again, why not give everyone a big headache for an hour a day? If the only worry is that in a perfect world we wouldn't have a conception of goodness, the daily headache would take care of it. No need for famines or earthquakes.

GENE: Or if you're so worried about people failing to appreciate the good life, why not just give them nightmares. Have you ever awakened from a terrible dream and been so relieved that it was only a dream?

THEO: Absolutely. I keep hoping that's what will happen any moment now.

EVA: So, God could give us dreams. And why stop there? He's all-powerful. He could just snap His heavenly fingers and we'd all have the concepts of good and evil. He could snap His fingers again and no one would take his or her life for granted.

THEO: Okay, okay, I get it. Still, you've got to admit that if the world were as you say—if no serious suffering happened except in nightmares or during daily headache hours—then life would lose its drama. There'd be no heroism, no genuine danger or cause for fear. It would be a pretty colorless world. Think of your favorite book or movie. Whatever it is, what would remain of it if there weren't any true risk of harm or adversity to be overcome?

GENE: Good point. *Casablanca* probably wouldn't be such a powerful film if the Nazis were just a bad nightmare.

EVA: Oh, come on. Surely you'd trade *Casablanca* to prevent the Holocaust!

GENE: But it's not just *Casablanca*. What about the tragedies of Shakespeare, the operas of Verdi, the films of Spielberg? Those would go down the toilet, too.

EVA: Nice list. Steven Spielberg: Shakespeare of the silver screen!

THEO: Enough, children. Anyway, it's a mistake to focus just on art and entertainment, as if the main point of evil were to generate box office receipts. It's part of many religious views, certainly mine, that our time on Earth is just an instant compared to what lies thereafter. But our earthly existence isn't just for fun. It's then when we show our moral worth—when we earn our way into paradise. The world is a sort of moral obstacle course, full of opportunities for moral development. It has its share of pain and suffering, but what sort of obstacle course would it be if there weren't obstacles?

EVA: But why do we need obstacles? Why throw us in the middle of an obstacle course?

THEO: Because without it there'd be no moral development, no chance for the triumph of the human spirit, and no progress. The world would just be a boring, static place.

GENE: What you're saying sounds pretty compelling, Theo. As strange as it is to say, the world would be awfully bland without evil—natural or otherwise.

THEO: You mean you're actually conceding something? Pinch me!

GENE: Hold on, let's think about this more. Aren't we judging the blandness of the world we're imagining from the comfortable perspective of the well off? I mean, sure, from the mountaintop the ravages of war and the whole of human suffering can seem sweeping and grand. But what about the perspective of those who actually suffer and die? You'd probably have a hard time convincing the moaning child who can barely see out of his own filth that his suffering is worth it to add to the drama.

EVA: Right. It's one thing to lecture in loafers about the obstacle course facing you. It's quite another to be crushed by the obstacles, drowned by the floods, and murdered by bloodthirsty lunatics.

THEO: That's true. But the harms that befall those poor souls provide opportunities for others to show their worth.

EVA: That's so callous. News flash: the world isn't just a moral training camp for Theo. And if it were, that'd be totally unjust.

THEO: I'm not saying that. I don't know God's plan. I doubt any of us can even grasp it. But that doesn't mean I have to bow my head and say, "There must be no purpose to everything, so God doesn't exist." You say

God wouldn't have created a world with so much suffering. I just don't see how we could know that, especially since all we know is what we find in this life.

Eva: So you're saying the scales could all even out in the afterlife?

Theo: Sure, for all we know. Granted, those children who die of hunger or drown in tsunamis haven't had anything but suffering in this life. But I believe that this isn't the end for them. They might return to Earth as Rockefellers or they might occupy a particularly resplendent part of the afterlife.

Eva: So you're into reincarnation now? That doesn't seem very Christian.

Theo: I'm saying that we don't know God's plan. I don't believe in reincarnation, but I'd sooner change my mind about that than deny that God exists or say He puts innocent children through such misery without giving them anything in return.

Gene: So let me get clear on what you're saying. You're responding to the argument from evil by denying premise 2. On your view, there's no needless suffering in the world.

Theo: That's right, though my response to that premise has two parts. First, a lot of evil results from our misusing our free will. God would certainly prefer that this suffering not occur, but it's unavoidable—it's the price of making us free.

Gene: But then there's the evil that isn't caused by humans…

Theo: Right, but that too is unavoidable. The alternatives would be worse overall. It doesn't always seem that way to us, what with natural disasters and such. But that just shows that we're finite creatures. There's much that figures into God's overall plan that we can't comprehend. That's part two.

Eva: Part two seems like a stretch.

Theo: True, but again, we aren't privy to the big picture. You can't rule out the possibility that all the floods and earthquakes are vital components in an overall package that's better than all the alternatives. God has a purpose for everything that happens in nature.

Gene: I'm inclined to agree with Theo here, Eva. I've seen plenty of movies that didn't make sense to me until the end. Sometimes strange things happen that don't make sense until much, much later. Have you ever seen *The Wire*?

EVA: What, the HBO show?

GENE: Yeah, that's the one. Early in each season stuff happens that you barely notice or that seems pointless. But by the end of the season, everything fits into place, and you realize the significance of all that seemingly pointless stuff. The real world is much more complicated than a movie or TV series and God, if He exists, would be much more sophisticated than even the greatest director. So, how can I be certain that in the end, from some point of view this won't all make sense?

THEO: You can't.

EVA: Okay, look.

GENE: Can you stop clenching your fists, Eva?

THEO: She's clenching her fists?

GENE: Her knuckles are white.

EVA: Okay, okay. I'll chill out.

GENE: Good.

EVA: But you guys are both making a huge mistake.

THEO: Oh my God! Is that a threat? Gene, does she have a gun?

GENE: No, she looks a little pale, but then she always does.

EVA: No, I mean you guys are making an intellectual mistake.

GENE: It wouldn't be the first time.

EVA: Your mistake is to think that this is about certainty.

THEO: You seem pretty certain.

EVA: My point is that atheism doesn't imply that you think there's no conceivable way there could be a god with some Rube Goldberg–like plan that explains how all the suffering in the world winds up doing some good.

THEO: Rube Goldberg?

GENE: You know, a Rube Goldberg machine.

THEO: Oh thanks, that's really helpful. A Rube Goldberg *machine*. I though you meant a Rube Goldberg *hamster*.

EVA: Gene, explain what a Rube Goldberg machine is.

GENE: A Rube Goldberg machine is a ridiculously, unnecessarily complex contraption.

EVA: The point is that atheists needn't say we're 100% certain we're right. We say only that there's at least sufficient reason to conclude that God doesn't exist.

THEO: I deny that.

EVA: And I think you're still demanding too much of the atheist. On your view, she's got to say that God isn't even conceivable. That's too strong.

GENE: I'm surprised to hear you say that, Miss Conviction.

EVA: Let me give you an example. Suppose some people are on an ocean cruise.

THEO: Good, a cruise. As long as it's not a cross-country drive.

EVA: And suppose they've never seen the ship's captain.

GENE: They can't get to the bridge?

EVA: The bridge?

THEO: It's where the captain steers the ship.

EVA: I'll take your word for it. No, no one can get to the bridge, and no one can see in there either.

GENE: Okay.

EVA: Now let's suppose that the ship begins to turn towards an iceberg.

THEO: I think I've seen this movie. Have I seen this movie?

EVA: No. This ship turns toward an iceberg in the middle of the day.

THEO: Oh, okay.

EVA: It hits the iceberg, and all hell breaks loose. People fall overboard and drown, old men have heart attacks...

GENE: And the ship sinks.

EVA: No, curiously enough, the ship doesn't sink.

THEO: It was a glancing blow?

EVA: Right. The ship heads on into the ocean. Still no sign of the captain. And soon it becomes clear that the ship is going in very wide circles.

GENE: I haven't seen this movie, but I'd like to. Are there snakes in the bilge?

EVA: No, no snakes. But a debate starts on the ship. Some think there's no captain on board. Maybe the captain fell overboard or maybe she never boarded, but anyway there's no captain present, in their opinion.

Others think there's a perfectly able captain, who's doing all this ramming and turning for a reason. They don't know the reason, but they think one exists.

GENE: Isn't there another possibility? The captain might be drunk.

EVA: That's a possibility, but let's put that aside for the moment. So there are two groups: those who believe a captain is on board and those who believe there is no captain on board. Which group is the more reasonable?

GENE: The nonbelievers, obviously.

THEO: It depends on what other evidence there is.

EVA: Okay, let's suppose during the voyage the boat runs over a smaller boat, crushing the people inside; that it has another collision, this time with a rocky shore; and that its course is zigzaggy, sometimes turning, sometimes straight.

THEO: Okay, there's probably no captain.

EVA: But wait! The captain believers protest: how do we know that this isn't all part of the captain's plan? Maybe the ship turned into the iceberg because it was dodging a mine, and maybe the boat it ran over was an enemy ship, out to plant mines, and maybe the circles are to confuse the enemy...

THEO: Okay, I get it.

EVA: And maybe not only is there a captain, but this is one James Bond of a perfect captain, steering the ship deftly under dire circumstances!

THEO: I said I got it.

EVA: You can't rule that out!

GENE: Okay, Eva. Enough already.

EVA: The point is that you don't have to rule out, with absolute, indubitable certainty every other hypothesis to know which hypothesis is the most reasonable, or to accept a hypothesis as established.

GENE: It's a good point. But I still think there should have been some snakes in the bilge.

THEO: I don't buy your analogy, Eva.

EVA: No surprise there.

THEO: People go on cruises for certain reasons, with certain expectations, and captains have a specific job. In your case, these people know that job isn't being done correctly.

EVA: Are they certain? Granted, this is no normal cruise. But how do they know for sure that the captain hasn't been made aware of a complicated, evil plot—one he's doing his best to foil?

GENE: I don't know why you're ignoring the obvious possibility: the captain is drunk.

THEO: I'm not crazy about that possibility.

GENE: Why not? It seems the most likely.

THEO: Because the analogous position is that God is incompetent.

EVA: Right. And the drunk-captain theory is plausible only because the believers know that ships typically have captains. We don't have anything like that in the God case. So instead of thinking we have a drunk, incompetent God, we should just conclude that the world arose naturally and that God is a superstition.

THEO: Or we could just take God's plan on faith and humbly admit our ignorance. For example, neither of you probably noticed that we're not in Kansas anymore.

GENE: No, Dorothy? Where are we?

THEO: Colorado! In fact, Denver's not far.

EVA: And after Denver...

THEO: Vegas, Baby! Vegas!

8
Las Vegas, Nevada

Pascal's Wager

THEO: Vegas, Baby! Vegas!

EVA: [*groggily*] Theo, aren't you tired? Don't you need to sleep?

THEO: Sleeping don't roll dice, baby! No sleeping in Vegas!

EVA: Would you please stop calling everyone "baby"?

GENE: And turn off that Sinatra. Or turn it down, at least.

THEO: Hey man, that's the Chairman of the Board! Old Blue Eyes!

GENE: Whatever. Just shut it off. Every time I hear that guy I feel like someone's about to get "whacked."

EVA: Wow. You know, it's a pretty impressive sight. It's like we're rolling into Babylon.

THEO: Babylon, baby! Babylon!

EVA: Seriously, cut it out.

GENE: Can we stop somewhere for coffee? I don't even think our room will be available yet.

EVA: Where are we staying again?

THEO: Vatican City.

EVA: I can't believe they made a casino out of the Vatican.

THEO: Judging from the pictures, it's a pretty good replica. I wouldn't expect to see the Pope, though.

143

GENE: There's a coffee shop! "Wide-Eyed Jacks!" Pull over.

EVA: Wow. Valet parking at a coffee shop.

Theo hands the keys over to a zealous parking attendant, and the three travelers stumble into the doors of Wide-Eyed Jacks. After getting their ultra-caffeinated beverages, they settle into a booth with a table painted like a roulette wheel.

GENE: Man, absolutely everything is gambling themed.

EVA: Welcome to Vegas.

GENE: Are you guys really going to gamble?

THEO: Of course! I'm going to find me some poker!

EVA: Yeah, we probably won't be seeing much of Theo while we're here. I'm going to try my hand at the blackjack tables. I read about a way of counting that can give you a little edge.

GENE: Careful, Eva. You'll need those fingers to type your papers in grad school.

EVA: I don't think I'm going to break any banks at the one-dollar tables, but thanks for the tip. What about you, Gene?

GENE: I'll probably just watch you guys. Maybe I'll play some slots.

THEO: Aw, that's just throwing your money away, man.

GENE: Maybe so, but it's not quite so high-pressure. And I can rack up on the free drinks.

EVA: Careful. You don't want a repeat of Chicago.

GENE: No, I don't. Hey, do you think they have God slots in the Vatican Casino?

THEO: I don't even know what that would mean.

EVA: Instead of cherries, bars, and sevens, you try to line up crosses, crescent moons, and stars of David?

THEO: Cute.

GENE: I'll bet they have that somewhere. You laugh, but I'll bet they do.

EVA: Actually, betting on religion has a long pedigree.

GENE: That's right. As in Pascal's wager, for example.

EVA: Right.

THEO: I've always thought that was a pretty bad reason to believe.

EVA: Me too.

GENE: Really? I think it's pretty convincing. It's a theological tie-breaker.

EVA: You need to think again.

GENE: Maybe we understand Pascal's argument differently.

THEO: Well, the reasoning is pretty straightforward. God is a good bet. If you believe in God and you're right, you go to heaven. If you're wrong, not much happens. You just die. If you don't believe in God and you're right, nothing much happens. You just die. If you're wrong, though, you go to hell.

GENE: Yeah, that's my understanding too. Believing has fantastic benefits if you're right and comparatively little cost if you're wrong. By contrast, not believing has terrible costs if you're wrong and comparatively little benefit if you're right.

EVA: Right. And I think Pascal would agree with the tie-breaker characterization. He thought human beings are incapable of determining whether God exists. In his view, the arguments on both sides are all bound to fail. His wager argument seems to show that we should believe in God anyway. In that sense, the wager breaks the tie.

GENE: I pretty much agree with Pascal. The arguments for God's existence—at least those we've discussed—all seem to fall short of the mark. The argument from evil has considerable force. But in the end, I'm not convinced it works either. So, I don't know what to think. Pascal's argument might tip the balance in God's favor.

EVA: Actually, though, are these metaphors—tipping the balance, breaking the tie—apt? I'm having some doubts. There's something importantly different about this argument. It's not an argument that God exists. It's an argument that you should believe in His existence. It tries to convince you to believe something without providing evidence for it. That seems odd.

GENE: Odd but not unheard of. It's just offering a different sort of reason to believe something—a prudential reason, instead of evidence. They say hospital patients who believe they're going to get well tend to get well quicker than those who believe they're done for.

EVA: Yeah, I've heard that. I'd like to see the evidence.

GENE: Well, let's just assume those stories are true. If so, and if doctors know about them, then there are two different reasons a doctor might give a patient to believe he'll get better. She can point to blood tests and x-rays, saying that the tests indicate that he'll recover soon.

EVA: Give him evidence, in other words.

GENE: Right. Or she could admit that the signs are bad, but tell the patient there's still a reason to believe he'll recover, namely, believing it will improve his prospects.

EVA: I'd have a hard time with that doctor. If she wanted me to believe I was getting better, she should have lied to me.

THEO: Gene, isn't it kind of like saying, "Here's a reason to love me: love me or I'll cut your throat!"? How could that work?

GENE: That's not the right kind of reason in the case of love. But it's still a reason. And by Pascal's argument, I have a compelling reason to believe in God.

THEO: I'd welcome your conversion, Gene. Unfortunately, the wager has problems.

GENE: I'm listening.

THEO: I'm not sure you can get yourself to believe something just because you have an incentive to do so.

GENE: Why not?

THEO: What we believe is not up to us in the sense that would require. Consider another example. I'm sure it would help my confidence to believe I'm the smartest person in every room. But I can't believe that, no matter how much I'd like to. There's simply too much evidence to the contrary.

EVA: No kidding.

THEO: And we can't just start believing that Eva is tall, even though she might like for us to. She's not tall, and we can't help seeing that.

GENE: I agree. I couldn't believe Eva is tall if my life depended on it.

EVA: Okay, enough of that.

GENE: Actually, though, people can get themselves to believe in all sorts of things for prudential reasons. Take my cousin Stephen. He was scared of dogs when he was a kid, and we had a German Shepherd.

EVA: I hope you didn't like your cousin.

GENE: It was a real problem. When I had birthday parties, Stephen wouldn't want to come. When he'd walk through the front gate and see Mozart, he'd start panicking. That got her excited, which made her jump on Stephen.

Eva: "Mozart"?

Theo: Mozart was Austrian, wasn't he?

Gene: Look, the dog's name isn't important. Anyway, we told Stephen that Mozart attacked because she smelled his fear.

Eva: Oh, I'm sure that made him feel better.

Gene: Well, we also told him to believe that we didn't have a dog—that instead we had a statue of a dog. Then we'd tell Mozart to sit before he got out of the car. From then on, as long as he could convince himself that the thing in the corner of his eye was just a statue, he could get to the house unharmed. And it worked!

Theo: Couldn't you have just tied the damn dog up?

Gene: I suppose we could have. Maybe my parents were anti-leash. I don't remember.

Theo: What a family. Anyway, even if you can sometimes get yourself to believe something for purely prudential reasons, I'm not sure you could get yourself to believe in God just because you think doing so is in your self-interest. Plus, if you could pull that off, God would see right through it. He'd know that you're believing only to save your own skin.

Eva: So?

Theo: So, He might not count your belief as genuine—as the kind that gets you through the Pearly Gates.

Gene: I don't see why He wouldn't. Sure, just saying that you believe doesn't guarantee that you do. But I think self-interest can produce genuine, heartfelt belief. Granted, when you first make the wager and decide to believe in God, your belief would be motivated by prudence. But then let's say you start going to church, socializing with believers, reading the Bible, and praying. Over time, your belief might be as sincere as anyone's.

Theo: Maybe, but your belief would still be based on the wrong reasons.

Gene: Not necessarily. Don't confuse your reasons for initially trying to believe with those you come to develop after months or years of religious activity. Your reasons might eventually come to be indistinguishable from the rest of the flock.

Eva: I agree with Gene. Think about how most people come to worship God. As children, they worship because their parents and other authority figures tell them to. But that's not the way it usually ends up. Eventually they worship because they believe in and love God.

GENE: Right. And think of couples in India who have their marriages arranged. These people may have met only once before getting married. Their relationship exists entirely because their parents set it up. I doubt many expect them to fall in love right away. But in most cases, affection develops over time. Through shared experiences, they develop a bond that's independent of their parents' wills and becomes, quite probably, true love.

THEO: So you're saying that God would forgive the prudential reasons you entered into the relationship with him and embrace you, so long as the love and faith you have at the moment are genuine.

GENE: Right. If He accepts the love of people who started believing because of their upbringing, He should also accept the love of Pascal's wagerers.

THEO: This wagering business still seems fishy to me. But I'll let it pass.

GENE: And if you do, we've got a pretty compelling reason for belief.

EVA: Nope.

GENE: Nope? Why nope?

EVA: I don't think the logic of this argument works out quite as cleanly as you think.

GENE: It looks good to me. It's based on the idea that sometimes one course of action is better than another course of action no matter what happens.

THEO: Right. That's called dominance. It's an important concept in poker. Sometimes you have a hand that you know will win, no matter which card is turned next. Or more often, you have a crappy hand, but you might be hoping for a particular card, which would give you a straight. The problem is that, in some cases, if that card falls it will give your opponent a flush, a better hand. If so, then you lose no matter what card is dealt. Your hand is dominated.

GENE: So, the card that would give you a straight is also in your opponent's hand?

THEO: Right. In Texas Hold 'Em, some cards are in every player's hand.

EVA: So how does this relate to Pascal again?

GENE: He says believing in God dominates not believing in God. If it turns out that God exists, the believer winds up much better off than the nonbeliever—infinitely better off, in fact.

Eva: Infinitely?

Gene: Don't forget the "eternal" in eternal happiness.

Theo: Or in eternal damnation. And by contrast, the things you gain by not believing—sleeping in on Sundays for example—are all finite.

Eva: Ah, right.

Gene: And if it turns out that God doesn't exist, the believer is at least no worse off.

Theo: Actually, the believer is still better off. She has the comforts provided by belief during her lifetime. And if her belief turns out to be false, she won't be around to be disappointed. So, there's no significant downside.

Eva: That's totally wrong. I like sleeping in on Sunday. Missing out on that would be a serious sacrifice. And then there's the obvious downside: having false beliefs!

Theo: Having false beliefs isn't so painful if you never realize it.

Gene: So what's wrong with the argument's logic? Seems like a simple case of dominance.

Eva: Okay, maybe the logic isn't the problem, strictly speaking. My point is that the reasoning is deceptively simple. You need to look closer.

Gene: I'm looking…

Eva: Let me give you an analogy. My uncle Rick is a member of the NRA. He collects guns, has a permit to carry a concealed weapon, the whole nine yards.

Gene: Okay, so don't mess with Uncle Rick. What else have we learned here?

Eva: Bear with me. So, on the other side of the coin, my father is a big gun control fanatic. He'd be happy if guns were totally banned.

Theo: I suppose that makes for some tricky Thanksgivings.

Eva: Yeah, they argue about it every time. It's almost a tradition. Anyway, Uncle Rick has a saying about carrying a gun: "Better to have it and not need it than to need it and not have it."

Gene: I've heard that. It's not a bad argument.

Theo: It's the same sort of dominance argument. Having a gun dominates not having a gun, since at worst you just never have to use it, but at best it will save your life.

EVA: That's right, it's the same argument, and it's bad in exactly the same way.

GENE: Explain.

EVA: Well, it looks like owning a gun is the dominant option only because you're considering a small number of cases. You're ignoring lots of scenarios where having a gun is a really bad idea. Like when your four-year-old finds it loaded, and when you're drunk and depressed, or raging mad. And when you're creeped out late at night and your husband comes home early from a business trip.

THEO: And like not needing it when your attacker overpowers you and shoots you with your own gun instead of just taking your money or hitting you.

GENE: That's right. I read some statistic that people with guns are more likely to die by their own guns than by the guns of attackers.

EVA: My uncle disputes those statistics. He says that, with respect to security risks, the benefits of carrying a gun far outweigh the costs, as long as you're a stable, trained gun owner. He cites statistics to back that claim up. He may be wrong: I don't know. But the point is that owning a gun is no longer simply a dominant option. It has downsides in scenarios that you weren't paying attention to. Serious downsides. How likely those scenarios are might be an open question. But that's the point: now we see that the rationality of carrying a gun depends on empirical questions about statistics and gun safety. The simple dominance argument doesn't work.

GENE: Fair enough. I assume you're going to say we're overlooking some scenarios in the God case as well.

EVA: Yep. Pascal considers four scenarios: you believe God exists and He does; you believe He exists and He doesn't; you don't believe He exists and He does; and finally, you don't believe He exists and He doesn't. Those may seem to exhaust the possibilities. But here's the thing. In all four cases, the assumption is that it's the Christian God who does or doesn't exist: the God who rewards Christian believers with heaven and who punishes others with hell. There are other possibilities.

THEO: Such as?

EVA: Suppose the god who exists hates Christians. She sends Christian believers to hell.

THEO: What are you talking about? Such a being would not be God.

EVA: Nonetheless, some people believe in such a god. You might not want to call her "God," but how can we rule out that she exists? This would be a sort of rationalist god, with a fondness for skeptics. She deplores those who take things on faith or believe things that run contrary to the evidence. She takes offense that such people are flouting their god-given rational faculties and the evidence of their senses. She punishes believers with hell. And she rewards atheists with heaven for following the evidence where it leads.

GENE: That would be pretty wily.

THEO: Yeah, but what are the chances of such alternative gods existing? This scenario seems outlandish.

EVA: Well, first of all, notice that now this is no longer a simple dominance argument. The case for betting on God now depends on independent evidence that your preferred god is more likely to exist than the others. Pascal's wager was supposed to be a tie-breaker—to give a reason to believe in God in spite of the alleged fact that the evidence doesn't point conclusively one way or the other. But if the wager is useless unless you have good evidence for the existence or nonexistence of certain gods over others, then it seems pretty, well, useless.

GENE: I'm not sure it's completely useless. You might not have conclusive evidence that there's one god rather than another, but if you have evidence that the Judeo-Christian God is significantly more likely to exist than any other god, then the wager could still do some work.

EVA: If you have good evidence for the existence of the Judeo-Christian God, then you should base your belief on that evidence. The wager doesn't enter into it.

GENE: But you might have evidence that *if* some god exists He's more like the Christian God than, say, the rationalist god.

EVA: Okay, that's true. If you were in that situation the wager might still be of some use. But why think we're in that situation? Didn't we agree that the arguments we discussed don't show too much about what God is like?

THEO: There's some truth in that. The cosmological argument tries to show that there's a god that created the universe, and the design arguments try to show that there's a god that intentionally designed the universe or certain aspects of it. Those arguments, if sound, wouldn't go all the way towards establishing the existence of the Judeo-Christian God. But the ontological argument would show that there's a perfect god.

EVA: That doesn't help much.

THEO: Why not? The god I believe in is perfect.

EVA: But you don't know what a perfect god is like. In particular, you don't know what sort of people, if any, a perfect god would look kindly on. A perfect god might be the rationalist god.

GENE: You might think the fact that no one believes in the rationalist god and many people believe in other sorts of gods is evidence.

EVA: Are you kidding? The whole point of a rationalist god is that he punishes believers. Of course you're not going to find anyone believing in him! That'd be like sending yourself to hell!

GENE: Still, there are texts and stories about the Judeo-Christian God. Not about the rationalist god.

EVA: In one sense, that's not surprising. In some ways, it's even untrue. Science itself could be seen as a sort of rationalist institution. In any case, the rationalist god was just one example. There are certainly texts describing gods that wouldn't look favorably on worshipers of the Christian faith.

GENE: I don't suppose Zeus or the Greek gods would have much affection for Christians.

EVA: No, and on some readings of the Qur'an, Christians don't wind up doing so well. Even if a group of people believing something is evidence of its truth, that doesn't help much. The competing claims of religions are enough to mess up Pascal's wager. For just about any religion you choose, there are people who believe in a scenario that lands you in hell.

GENE: Okay, maybe Pascal's wager isn't such a good bet.

THEO: Yeah, I guess I side with Eva on this one.

EVA: Alright! Theo and I agree!

THEO: Speaking of which, what do you say we hit the tables real quick before we go to our hotels?

EVA: What tables?

THEO: Haven't you noticed the ones in the back of the coffee shop?

EVA: Oh, yeah. With the dealer who looks like Elvis?

THEO: That's the one.

EVA: I'm game. You coming, Gene?

GENE: I think we've seen my talent for gambling. I'll just watch you guys.

THEO: Have it your way. Let's go, Eva! Baby needs a new pair of shoes!

EVA: What does that even mean?

THEO: I don't know. Just play along, okay?

EVA: Just this once.

9
California

Faith and the Rationality of Belief in God

THEO: California, here we come…

GENE: Finally! I was beginning to think California didn't exist.

THEO: I'm pretty sure there aren't any good arguments for that, at least.

GENE: I don't know about that. We've passed through a lot of states this trip. The next state has never been California. So, the next state will never be California. Simple induction! There are good arguments for all sides of every issue!

EVA: I think Hume is spinning in his grave.

THEO: Man, Gene. No wonder you're an agnostic!

EVA: You're not still an agnostic, are you Gene? After all these arguments? After the problem of evil and everything?

GENE: I'm afraid so. At least I think so.

THEO: Gene's an agnostic about his own agnosticism. Talk about indecisive.

GENE: It still seems like the right stance to me. There are arguments on both sides…

EVA: That's right. Bad arguments on one side, good arguments on the other! That's no reason for agnosticism!

THEO: I don't usually agree with Eva, but in this case I do.

EVA: You think the arguments for the existence of God are bad and those against are good?!

THEO: No, not that. But I don't think the sheer number of arguments on one side or the other tells you anything. After all, Gene just made an argument that California doesn't exist, and I'm sure one could make many others. That shows nothing.

GENE: Okay, I didn't mean that we should withhold belief just because there are arguments on both sides. But as I said earlier, the argument from evil is pretty strong. And there's something persuasive about the pro-God arguments, despite their shortcomings.

EVA: But each has a fatal flaw! At least one!

THEO: I'm not sure about that.

EVA: Well, should we go back over the arguments?

GENE AND THEO: No, no!

THEO: Spare us, Eva. We're almost there.

EVA: Fine. But Gene, can you tell me why even one of the pro-God arguments works, despite the problems we discussed?

GENE: It's not that there's one that I endorse. But I wonder if the way we've been approaching things is fair to theism. Maybe one argument in isolation doesn't prove that God exists, but taken together...

EVA: So though two wrongs don't make a right, two bad arguments can make a good one?

GENE: Not necessarily. But even if one argument doesn't fully establish a thesis, combining that argument with others might.

EVA: So, for example...?

GENE: Suppose you tell me a presidential candidate has the youth vote. That might not be enough reason for me to conclude she'll win. But if you tell me she has the youth vote and the senior vote, that might be enough reason.

THEO: So you're saying though each individual argument for God's existence fails, taken together they add up to a successful proof?

GENE: Something like that.

EVA: Alright, a couple of things about that. First, in your election case you do have a single argument that the candidate will win: if a candidate has both the youth and the senior vote, she's likely to win, and your candidate has both. There's nothing like that in the God case.

THEO: In other words, if two inconclusive arguments can supplement each other in the way Gene's example suggests, then there must be one conclusive argument that combines the premises of those arguments.

EVA: Exactly. And I don't see that logic applying to the arguments for theism. They don't seem to fit together in the right way.

GENE: Maybe that's right. I'm not sure.

EVA: Hold on, there's a second point that explains why the arguments for God's existence don't add in the way you're thinking they might. In all of them, we're implicitly comparing two hypotheses: a supernatural hypothesis involving God, and a naturalistic one that doesn't involve God. We never found the supernatural hypothesis to be more likely than the naturalistic one. So, it's not like the case of a candidate winning the youth vote and the senior vote. It's more like: candidate A trails candidate B in both the youth vote and the senior vote. That doesn't predict victory for candidate A.

GENE: Look, it just seems that these arguments build on each other in some way.

EVA: I'm not denying that. But there are different ways arguments can build on one another, and not all favor theism. Here's an analogy. A strong rope is made up of many different strands woven together. But that's not the only way those strands can be combined. They could be woven into a much longer rope if they were tied end to end, instead of woven together.

GENE: Then the rope would be longer but also weaker.

EVA: Right. And in the case of the pro-God arguments, I think we're dealing with a long, weak rope. Putting them together doesn't make a single argument that can support a lot of argumentative weight.

GENE: Neat analogy. A little vague, though.

THEO: I'm not sure it's accurate. But you know, I'm not sure how much any of this matters.

EVA: It doesn't matter much whether there's a supreme being hovering over our lives? *You* think that?

THEO: No, I mean I'm not sure how much the arguments matter.

GENE: Great. We've been analyzing the arguments since Plymouth Rock and they're insignificant? What a waste! I could have been boning up on Scrabble® words.

THEO: I'm not saying the arguments are futile. I just wonder whether they're needed. Maybe what it all comes down to is a leap of faith.

EVA: Ah, I was wondering when Kierkegaard would come into this.

GENE: Kierkegaard?

THEO: The Great Dane.

EVA: Søren Kierkegaard. Sometimes called the father of existentialism.

GENE: I thought the existentialists were atheists.

EVA: A lot of them were. But not Kierkegaard.

THEO: He's famous for suggesting that belief in God is absurd, in that it's contrary to reason, but that its absurdity is part of what makes it great. He said belief in God is heroic, because unlike so many things it requires a pure "leap of faith." In fact, the failure of all of these arguments against the existence of God, and the strength of the case against it, makes the leap all the more heroic.

EVA: I don't see what's heroic about it.

THEO: Well, to paraphrase another existentialist, it's like charging a nest of machine-guns in the midst of a battle. Acts of heroism are performed unreasonably, against all odds. If it were easy, it wouldn't be heroic.

EVA: Believing in God is like charging a nest of machine-guns. Gee, Gene, I don't see why you're reluctant to believe.

GENE: Actually, I do see something romantic in this leap of faith notion.

EVA: Really?

GENE: Sure. Reason has to run out somewhere, and I can see a certain strength in holding on even after it has.

EVA: Aghh!

THEO: Is she melting?

GENE: I think she is.

EVA: Okay, first of all, it doesn't follow that reason has "run out" just because you haven't been able to prove what you want to prove. In fact, I think the argument from evil shows pretty conclusively what we should believe.

GENE: I didn't find that conclusive. Provocative, definitely. Persuasive, maybe. But conclusive? No.

EVA: Okay, suppose that's right. Suppose we don't have good evidence against God's existence. Even so, it's just not rational to draw conclusions that reason doesn't support. Do you believe the number of stars is even rather than odd?

GENE: Of course not.

EVA: Okay, why?

GENE: I haven't counted them.

EVA: Right, and you aren't in a position to.

THEO: That's clearly different. Who cares about that?

EVA: You're right: it's different precisely because no one cares. But don't you think we should be even more careful when it comes to things that matter? Or is that the time to throw caution to the wind and make arbitrary decisions about what to believe?

THEO: Just because it's a leap of faith doesn't mean it's arbitrary.

EVA: I'm not so sure. Why leap one direction rather than another?

THEO: Well, have you heard any atheists describe themselves as taking a leap of faith?

GENE: Maybe they wouldn't put it that way, but the point's the same. If they conclude that God doesn't exist, as opposed to being either theistic or agnostic, then they're taking a leap of faith in God's nonexistence.

EVA: Unless they buy the argument from evil.

GENE: Right. Or some other argument against God's existence. Or for agnosticism.

EVA: Right. But put that aside. There's another problem for taking a leap of faith in the sense Theo means.

GENE: Do you mean: for having faith in God's existence, despite having no good arguments for it?

EVA: Exactly. So, suppose you decide to take that leap of faith. Which conception of God should you embrace? Which prophet should you follow? If reason isn't there to guide you, what keeps you from following the gods of the Hindus or Greeks? For that matter, what keeps you from following Hitler?

THEO: Oh, come on.

EVA: No, I'm serious. I think it's dangerous to abandon reason and follow something based on faith—whether the thing is a religion, an ideology, a supernatural god, or a flesh-and-bones tyrant. In the 1930's and 40's, plenty of people had faith in the Führer. I doubt too many did so because they were convinced by the perverse reasoning of his book, *Mein Kampf.*

THEO: Maybe, but that comparison is unfair and offensive. Believing in God isn't anything like following Hitler. In believing in God, I'm not just mindlessly endorsing the vile notion that entire classes of people should be extinguished.

EVA: True, you're not. But history has no shortage of people who do. And they endorse that notion under the guise of faith in God—from the Christian crusaders to the radical fundamentalists of Al-Qaida.

THEO: Maybe so. But the problem isn't their leap of faith. It's their intolerance.

EVA: No, you're missing the point. Those people are just making a different leap. It's a less friendly, more intolerant god, but it's still a leap. Why think one leap is more legitimate than another? If it's faith, it's beyond reason, by definition. So, how can you rationally criticize their faith in a way that wouldn't undermine the legitimacy of your own?

THEO: I can criticize them from the perspective of my beliefs.

EVA: And they can criticize you from the perspective of theirs.

THEO: Look, this is just unfair. The Nazis didn't try to justify genocide with religion. They appealed to natural selection!

GENE: Okay, guys. Chill out. No need to compare each other to the Nazis.

THEO: Okay, sorry.

EVA: Yeah, sorry. But you see my point, don't you, Gene?

GENE: Yeah, but I can see things from Theo's perspective as well.

THEO: Of course! Ever the agnostic!

GENE: Still, I'm sort of surprised, Theo, at the fact that you characterize your belief as a leap of faith.

THEO: I'm not saying it's completely a leap of faith. That's just part of it.

GENE: I thought so. Back in Iowa you did seem to think you were justified in believing on the basis of your religious experiences.

THEO: That's right. That's part of it too.

GENE: I'm not sure those parts fit together too well.

THEO: Why not?

GENE: Faith is supposed to be heroic because it extends beyond reason. That suggests that God wants us to believe without evidence, or even against the evidence. Yet you think He does provide evidence in the form of religious revelations.

EVA: Not to mention prophets who claim to carry the word of God. Like Moses. And Jesus.

THEO: Wait, what's the problem, exactly?

GENE: The problem is reconciling revelations with faith. Why does God provide us with evidence for His existence—revelations—if He doesn't want us to use that evidence in deciding whether to believe? And if He does want us to use evidence here, why doesn't He give us a lot more evidence than He does?

EVA: Yeah, I see the tension. Theo, you're trying to have it both ways.

THEO: I don't see why that's bad. Suppose you have a husband who says he loves you and is faithful to you.

GENE: Is that legal in California? I thought it wasn't.

THEO: I meant suppose *Eva* has a husband. But whatever.

EVA: Okay, so he seems faithful but in fact he's not?

THEO: You don't know for sure, do you? When he's on business trips he calls you at night before he goes to bed, so he gives you some evidence that he's thinking of you. But that evidence doesn't rule out the possibility of infidelity.

EVA: True. But why would he cheat? I mean, I'm gorgeous.

THEO: And modest too! Anyway, it's perfectly reasonable for him to resist putting a video camera in his hotel room to prove he's alone. Being such a skeptic, you might want him to do that. But if you lack faith to that degree there's something wrong, isn't there?

EVA: Yeah, that makes sense.

THEO: So, there's a place for evidence, and a place for faith. No conflict.

GENE: Interesting. Still, I feel as though I'm not getting enough phone calls to allay my doubts.

THEO: Maybe that's because you haven't been paying your phone bill.

EVA: Oh, God! Yuck! Enough with the evangelical analogies!

THEO: What's good for the goose is good for the gander!

EVA: Okay, okay. But Gene makes a good point. Why would God give us the gift of reason, the drive to scientific explanation, the itch to find reasons, if He ultimately just wants us to throw it all away when it comes to belief in Him?

THEO: I don't believe He does. I think God wants us to remain reasonable in our belief.

EVA: Despite the fact that He wants us to believe without sufficient evidence.

THEO: Despite the fact that He wants us to believe without *conclusive* evidence.

EVA: I don't ask for conclusive evidence. I just see no evidence at all.

GENE: Okay, we're back to that. I agree with you, Eva, to some extent. I don't see sufficient reason to believe based solely on evidence. And you're right, one has to be careful with leaps of faith. But I wonder why there couldn't be other reasons to believe—reasons that don't stem from argument or evidence, or at least perception.

EVA: How can there be reasons without evidence for the truth of the belief?

THEO: We talked about this in Vegas. The patient who believes in order to have hope. Your cousin who believed Mozart the dog was a statue to get over his fear of dogs. Remember?

EVA: Yeah, okay, right. But I'm not sure the point applies here.

GENE: It might. I know people who go to church, believe, and generally lead a religious life ultimately because it makes them feel better. I mean, that's not what they say when you ask why they believe, but I think it might be the truth.

THEO: Some people are quite explicit about it. I have an aunt who started going to church soon after her husband died. Even though she's really quite pious, she says it provided a sort of comfort she needed at that point in her life.

EVA: To me that sounds like intellectual cowardice.

GENE: That's a little harsh, Eva. We all have our illusions.

THEO: But I don't think these are just illusions. It's not as though the faithful have imaginary friends they think are real.

EVA: I don't know, it seems a bit like that to me.

THEO: That's overly simplistic. Many religious people don't believe there's some bearded old man sitting on a throne in the clouds—which isn't what I believe either, by the way.

EVA: What's the alternative?

THEO: There's more than one. Some highly sophisticated theologians believe that God is a simple and unchanging being that exists outside of space and time. Other scholars believe that He is a sort of presence that should be closely identified with nature or even the deep structure of the natural world. There are all sorts of sophisticated views out there.

EVA: Yeah, I hear philosophers say things like that. But I usually don't know what they mean. This reminds me of my Aunt Margie who insists that she has children—they're her cats! If you let "God" mean just anything, I guess I could believe in God. For example, if you identify God with the laws of nature, then consider me on board.

THEO: Now we have a conversion!

EVA: Hardly. I mean, of course I believe in the laws of nature, and if someone wants to call those "God," more power to him. But that so-called god wouldn't be the sort of thing that answers prayers, cares about humans, makes decisions, or has intentions. Such a god wouldn't have any mental life at all. Surely, when we talk ordinarily about God, we mean a being with all of those properties at least. Not some Platonic form or nonsentient matter that existed at the beginning of the universe. To my mind, when you characterize God in those sorts of ways, you're changing the subject.

GENE: You've gotta admit, Theo, that's not the sort of thing you seemed to be talking about back in Iowa. You spoke about a being that provides comfort and love.

THEO: Perhaps, although I'm not willing to ditch the theologians just yet. Besides, there's another tack that some religious people take. For them, religion encodes a set of deeply held values, and their belief in God is a sort of affirmation of those values. It's not that they believe in some bearded spirit king. For them, religious images of that sort are metaphorical.

EVA: Metaphorical?

THEO: In a way.

EVA: So these people don't really believe Jesus is the son of God, the product of a virgin birth?

THEO: Well, you'd have to ask them. I believe Jesus was literally God's son. Still, I can see someone professing those beliefs but only as a way of acknowledging the existence of a higher power and as a way of indicating that some things transcend her understanding.

GENE: So on this belief-as-metaphor view, what exactly is God a metaphor for?

THEO: I suspect it varies, but the most obvious candidate is *goodness* or something like that. I'm not sure it has to be cashed out so explicitly. Belief in God is, for some, a way of expressing belief in the benevolence of the universe—in the fact that there's such a thing as objective goodness out there.

GENE: It's not obvious to me that the universe is all that benevolent. Remember all the children dying of hunger?

EVA: Every five seconds…

THEO: Even so, you can see how in the face of that, people need something to believe in, something to grab hold of.

EVA: I have to say, I'm not sure I understand this belief-as-metaphor business. Thinking of something as a metaphor seems to imply *not* believing it. I might believe Jack and the Beanstalk illustrates the idea that good can come from unexpected places. But I don't take the story as an account of something that actually happened. It's only a metaphor. It's because I recognize that fact that I don't infer from the story that magic beans exist.

GENE: I don't know. Some stories are so deeply ingrained in our culture that we almost take them literally. There's the notion of a Trojan horse, which might or might not have existed. But we can talk about it usefully to express the concept of a gift that's more dangerous than it first appears to be. You can imagine parents telling children to always be on the lookout for magic beans, as a way of telling them to keep an eye out for the surprising and unusual.

EVA: That's all fine, so long as the kids don't start frittering away their allowances on supposed magic beans. And so long as people don't start freaking out whenever someone gives them a horse for a present.

GENE: Yeah, that's a serious concern. People give me horses all the time. I'm gonna have to start re-gifting them soon. I'm running short of oats.

Eva: Look, the point is that the people who benefit from the metaphors have to know they're only metaphors, or else there might be trouble.

Theo: I'm not sure that's always true. Maybe some concepts, such as good and evil, are difficult to incorporate into your life without using some sort of metaphor.

Eva: This reminds me of when I was suspicious that Santa Claus didn't exist, and I asked my mother if she believed in Santa Claus. She replied by saying she believed in a spirit of love.

Gene: Aw, she gave up the game!

Eva: Yeah, I was like, "To hell with the spirit of love! If it doesn't wear a red suit and come down the chimney, it's not Santa!" I felt like it was a bait-and-switch. Don't you think a lot of people would feel that way if it turned out that all this God talk was just as metaphorical as Santa talk?

Theo: I'm not sure. I would, but some wouldn't.

Gene: I guess I don't see anything necessarily wrong with being religious in that way. But it does seem to have its dangers.

Eva: No kidding!

Theo: Like what?

Eva: Well, for one thing, if you go around talking about God and religion, and you don't make it clear that you're speaking metaphorically, people may take you literally. You'll be conveying something to them that you yourself don't believe.

Theo: You think it's like lying?

Eva: Maybe not exactly. You might not be intending to deceive anyone. But it's misleading. You'd be speaking in a way that will lead others to form false beliefs.

Gene: That can have some pretty dangerous side effects. When I was a kid I used to lay awake at night scared to death that I was going to hell.

Eva: And I have a gay cousin who was terrified of revealing his sexual orientation to his family when he was young.

Gene: Why?

Eva: Because they went to a pretty conservative church and said they believed in God. They seemed to buy into an ideology that was anti-gay. The preachers were clearly hostile to homosexuality. So my cousin assumed, reasonably enough, that his parents and siblings might reject him if he told them the truth.

GENE: Did he ever come out of closet?

EVA: Eventually.

GENE: What happened? Did they disown him?

EVA: Actually, no. For the most part, it seems everyone already knew. They were all sort of relieved—happy to be able to talk about it openly.

GENE: Cool. Those things don't always have such happy endings, though. Some people never come out of the closet or reveal their true selves because of the religion thing. They're afraid of being ostracized. And they're not being paranoid. Sadly, many people internalize those vile anti-gay sermons that your cousin probably had to endure. These lost souls take the anti-gay rhetoric at face value. Or they draw the wrong lessons from the metaphor. As a result, they don't embrace people who differ from them, but not in bad ways.

EVA: That's putting it mildly. The number of people who have been oppressed in the name of religion—this supposed metaphor—are legion! Homosexuals, women, atheists, people of color, people of other religions.... The list just goes on.

THEO: I'm not denying that some religious people and sects are intolerant and oppressive. But anything can be dangerous when taken to extremes. Science is no different. Just look to the gruesome pseudo-scientific medical experiments the Nazis performed. And what about the atomic bomb? Just because religion can be misused doesn't mean it's necessarily harmful. We shouldn't throw the baby out with the bathwater.

GENE: Okay, that's fair. We shouldn't paint an entire faith with the same brush that we paint its worst practitioners. But metaphors are still dangerous. They can lead to all sorts of error and confusion. They can contribute to the misuse of religion you're talking about.

THEO: I guess that's a legitimate concern. Remember, though, I myself don't buy the metaphor view.

GENE: I know, and I think that's more honest. At least you say what you mean and mean what you say.

EVA: But some of the dangers we've been discussing aren't associated only with the religion-as-metaphor view.

THEO: I don't espouse oppression or intolerance either. To me, God is all about love and peace.

EVA: Maybe so, but many associate your religion with things you abhor, such as anti-gay views. So, people may assume you're anti-gay even though you're not.

THEO: Sure, but that problem isn't distinctive to religion. People will sometimes assume you're pro-choice if they know you're a Democrat, even though lots of Democrats aren't pro-choice. There will always be some who misinterpret your beliefs.

EVA: True, but there's a related problem that stems from faith.

THEO: Go on.

EVA: You base your religious convictions on faith. But you don't accept everything associated with that religion. You pick and choose. On what basis do you do that? If your beliefs were based on reason and evidence, then there'd be no problem. But faith makes your selective approach seem arbitrary.

GENE: Hmm. That does seem bad.

EVA: Right. So, say you believe homosexuality is wrong.

THEO: What is with you? I *don't* believe that. Haven't I made that clear?

EVA: Okay, okay, sorry. So, say you believe—based on faith—that abortion is wrong.

THEO: Actually, I'm not sure what I think there. But okay, for the sake of argument, let's say I believe that on faith.

EVA: Now suppose someone else thinks that homosexuality should be outlawed. And a third person believes that polygamy should be legalized. All three of you hold your moral beliefs strongly. You all consider them part of the fabric of your faith.

THEO: Okay, I'm with you.

EVA: So, what puts you in a position to criticize the views of those other two people?

THEO: What do you mean? I can disagree with them as well as you can.

EVA: I'm not sure that's true. You can express disagreement, that's for sure. But what reasons can you provide? If your view bottoms out in faith, and their views also bottom out in faith, what can you say to them? Your views conflict, but each of you takes his view to reflect the word of God.

THEO: Well, I can explain why they're wrong about God's intentions. These people are interpreting the Bible perversely, in such a way that it involves oppression. I can show them where their interpretations go awry.

Eva: You're assuming the Bible lends itself to a single coherent interpretation—one that just happens to jibe with your egalitarian values. I'm skeptical about that.

Gene: You're also assuming you're both reading the Bible.

Eva: Right! What if they take a different book to indicate the word of God—one that contradicts the Bible?

Theo: I admit, at that point conversation would get pretty difficult. But don't you have the same problem? If you don't share some basic assumptions with the person you're talking to, what do you do?

Eva: The problem isn't so much about what I say in actual situations where I disagree with people. I mean, if someone is unwilling to reconsider their beliefs and assess them rationally, there's not much you can do. My concern is more with how I assess my own beliefs. If I know that the justification I have for my beliefs is essentially no different than the justification that someone else has—that God said so, for example—and yet our beliefs conflict, forget about persuading *them*. How do I persuade *myself* that I've got the right view?

Gene: And the problem is worse when it comes to making laws. How can you expect someone else to submit to a law—prohibiting homosexual sex, for example—when you know that your reasons for that prohibition ultimately depend on faith. By your own lights, faith isn't subject to rational criticism. *Your* having faith in something doesn't give *me* any reason to do or believe anything.

Theo: I see your point. But I still think you've got the same problem. For example, you probably have some moral beliefs that you just take to be self-evident. For example, causing me pain just because you happen to enjoy it would be wrong.

Eva: True.

Theo: So what's your basis for that?

Eva: Have you ever been in pain?

Theo: Yeah, I've had whipping headache for most of this trip.

Eva: Have you enjoyed it?

Theo: No, but what does that have to do with morality?

Eva: It seems pretty clear.

Theo: What if it seems otherwise to someone else? Aren't you back at just having two conflicting intuitions? What makes you think yours are better than theirs?

EVA: Oh, come on. There have to be standards for reasonableness. Someone who denies that pain is bad, all things considered, just isn't being rational.

GENE: Sometimes causing pain is okay because it serves some purpose. Don't they say, "No pain, no gain?"

EVA: Okay, right. But factor out that sort of consideration. Consider two hypothetical situations, A and B. A and B are exactly the same except for one thing: in A creatures suffer horrible pain, and in B they don't. B is surely better than A.

GENE: Morally?

EVA: Yes, morally.

GENE: What does that mean? Actions can be right and wrong. Can situations?

EVA: Well, it's all about value. And there are straightforward consequences for action. If you could bring about either situation and had to choose, you'd be morally required to choose B, other things being equal.

THEO: Says you!

GENE: I agree with Eva on A versus B. You don't?

THEO: *I* do, but suppose others don't. Who determines the standards? People will disagree about that. And then you're in the same boat I'm in. You can't justify your basic moral beliefs to those who don't share them any more than I can.

GENE: Eva's position seems a little more reasonable.

THEO: Than mine?

GENE: Well, it's more reasonable than someone who believes something just because they think God says so. I mean, Eva can demonstrate that pain is bad—even by the lights of someone who doesn't believe that.

THEO: Even a masochist?

GENE: I think even masochists probably have their limits. Just turn up the intensity of the pain enough and they'll probably stop longing to feel it.

THEO: Maybe. Maybe not.

EVA: If they don't, we're now talking about the lunatic fringe…

THEO: And who determines the fringe? You or them?

GENE: Okay, look. Let's grant for the sake of argument that at some point you reach rock-bottom in defending your views.

EVA: I guess there has to be such a point. Wittgenstein says that there's some point at which you have to say, "My spade is turned."

THEO: No more digging.

EVA: Right.

GENE: Okay, suppose that's true. Even so, some places are better than others for turning your spade. Suppose someone takes it as basic that there's nothing bad about pain as long as the creature feeling it is female or has red hair. That's not a good point to turn the spade … or to insist "that's just the way God wants it."

THEO: I agree.

EVA: But suppose someone adopts that attitude. If you base your values on God's edicts, then how can you prove you're right and that lunatic is wrong?

THEO: Maybe I can't. But again, I don't think my situation differs all that much from yours and Eva's. I'm not saying we should accept just any alleged case of "the word of God" and disregard what we know independently about what's right and what's wrong. Moral intuition doesn't disappear if you believe in God, and it shouldn't be ignored. After all, a believer should say that God gave you that moral intuition.

EVA: Ah, now we're getting somewhere. So you agree that one's judgment about what's moral should ultimately depend on intuition rather than God's word?

THEO: Sort of, but that's misleading. I think that our moral intuition is a good indication of what God's word probably is. This reminds me of our conversation back in Plymouth.

GENE: You mean about whether God says things are good because they are or the other way around? The *Euthyphro* thing?

THEO: Yeah. And I agreed then that we ultimately have to rely on our moral intuition. Things aren't good because God commands them—though I said God is still the source of goodness, because goodness is part of God.

EVA: So you don't think it would ever be correct to say "It's good because God said so?"

THEO: I wouldn't say never. But probably only in a context where I'm talking with someone who, like me, already accepts God as a moral judge.

EVA: Yeah, but in general you take your moral beliefs to be susceptible to rational criticism.

THEO: Do you think I'd have taken part in this conversation, from Plymouth to San Francisco, if I didn't?

EVA: Well, maybe.

THEO: Eva, how long have you known me? I think you assume that if someone is religious they must be unreasonable.

EVA: Well, on some level, yeah. I guess I do think that.

THEO: Jesus.

EVA: When it comes to him in particular, yes.

GENE: I can understand where you're coming from, Eva. But when faith plays the role it does in Theo's life, I'm not sure it's entirely unjustified.

THEO: Oh, thanks. I pass your bar but just barely?

GENE: I didn't mean it that way.

THEO: Then how did you mean it?

GENE: Sorry, I wasn't being clear. I'm still concerned about the baggage associated with religion. People can feel unsure of where to stand and unsure of whether they're going to be judged by standards they don't accept—standards based on something they can't question.

THEO: I can see that. But there are judgmental people on both sides of the fence. The problem isn't religious faith. The problem is being judgmental in inappropriate ways.

GENE: Like being anti-gay.

THEO: Right.

EVA: I'm not sure I think that's all there is here. You're acting like faith in God plays no role at all in how people believe and how they act. That can't be true. Otherwise there'd be nothing driving them to believe. But if faith does play a role, then there's something fundamentally nonrational at play when you're dealing with those people.

GENE: And that scares you.

EVA: It concerns me.

THEO: Don't worry Eva. I'm not going to burn you at the stake.

EVA: Thanks. That's reassuring.

GENE: Guess what else is reassuring?

THEO: San Francisco: ten miles!

EVA: Oh, thank God.

THEO: Don't say it if you don't mean it.

EVA: Aw, go to hell.

THEO: No, I think I'll check out the Mission first.

EVA: Of course. Drop me at Haight Street.

GENE: And I'll check out The Castro.

THEO: The Castro? What's in The Castro?

GENE: Ah, I just have a couple of friends there.

THEO: A couple of friends? What are we, chopped liver?

EVA: Let him be, Theo. He's at least committing to something. Speaking of which, shouldn't you have changed lanes back there?

THEO: I have an idea.

EVA: Another argument?

GENE: No, I absolutely refuse. No more arguments.

THEO: It's not an argument, but more of a point of view. Just bear with me.

EVA: We've been doing that since Plymouth Rock!

GENE: And it's going to be dark soon. Shouldn't we just call it a trip?

THEO: It's not dark yet. Look up ahead.

EVA: Oh my God! Park the car! Let's get out!

Theo parks the car, and the three of them run towards the Golden Gate Bridge where the falling sun is reflecting along the water and off the red of the towers.

THEO: See? Was this a good idea or what? The bridge at sunset!

EVA: It's beautiful.

GENE: One of the great engineering marvels.

EVA: Gives you faith in mankind.

THEO: It would be nothing without the sunset.

GENE: I see where this is going. Why don't we just be quiet and enjoy it?

EVA: Agreed.

THEO: Finally, agreement.

GENE: Shhhh.

Reading Suggestions

General

- David Hume's *Dialogues Concerning Natural Religion* (Indianapolis: Hackett Publishing Company, 1980; originally published in 1779) is a classic. A must read.
- Richard Swinburne's *The Existence of God*, second edition (New York: Oxford University Press, 2004; first edition published in 1979) is an influential defense of theism by a distinguished philosopher of religion.
- Graham R. Oppy's *Arguing about Gods* (New York: Cambridge University Press, 2006) is a detailed analysis of the main arguments concerning God's existence. Not an easy read, but rigorous and even handed.
- J. L. Mackie's *The Miracle of Theism* (Cambridge: Oxford University Press, 1982) is one of the best critical discussions of arguments for and against the existence of God.

1. Outside Boston: God, Value, and Meaning

- Jean Kaezez's *The Weight of Things: Philosophy and the Good Life* (Oxford: Blackwell Publishing, 2007) is accessible and thoughtful.
- In *Finite and Infinite Goods: A Framework for Ethics* (New York: Oxford University Press, 1999), Robert M. Adams develops a theistic framework for ethics. An important work by a distinguished philosopher.

- *James Rachels' The Elements of Moral Philosophy*, sixth edition, by Stuart Rachels (New York: McGraw-Hill, 2010; first edition published in 1986) is an accessible nontheistic introduction to ethics. Organized around the traditional moral theories, it includes a discussion of Divine Command Theory and the *Euthyphro* problem.

2. Niagara, New York: Design and Evolution

- The panda's thumb example comes from Stephen Jay Gould, "The Panda's Peculiar Thumb" (*Natural History, 87,* November 1978, pp. 20–30; reprinted in *The Panda's Thumb: More Reflections on Natural History*, New York: W. W. Norton & Company, Inc., 1980). A nice example of Gould's elegant writing on evolution.

- Biochemist Michael Behe updates Paley's design argument in his influential *Darwin's Black Box: The Biochemical Challenge to Evolution*, second edition (New York: Simon & Schuster, 2006; first edition published in 1996).

- In *Living with Darwin: Evolution, Design, and the Future of Faith* (New York: Oxford University Press, 2007), Philip Kitcher defends the theory of natural selection against recent attacks and explores the theory's implications for religious belief, among other things. Lucid and well informed.

- In *Finding Darwin's God: A Scientist's Search for Common Ground Between God and Evolution* (New York: HarperCollins, 1999), biologist Kenneth R. Miller defends evolution, criticizes intelligent design theory, and tries to reconcile evolution with theism.

- For Darwin's views on theism, and for clear-headed reflections on the moral implications of evolution, see James Rachels, *Created from Animals: The Moral Implications of Darwinism* (New York: Oxford University Press, 1990).

3. From Niagara to Chicago: Life and Fine-Tuning

- For a lucid, brief overview of research into the origins of life, see "Life on Earth," by Alonso Ricardo and Jack W. Szostak (*Scientific American*, September 2009, pp. 54–61). For a longer but still readable account by one of the scientists working in the trenches, see Robert M. Hazen's *Genesis: The Scientific Quest for Life's Origin* (Washington, DC: Joseph Henry Press, 2005).

- John Leslie's *Universes* (London: Routledge, 1989) provides a forceful presentation of the argument that fine-tuning considerations support the existence of multiple universes. It also contains a useful discussion of the so-called anthropic principle.
- Roger White gives a sophisticated criticism of the fine-tuning argument for multiple universes in "Fine-Tuning and Multiple Universes" (*Nous*, 34, 2000, pp. 260–276).
- For a rigorous discussion of the design argument, with special attention to fine tuning, see Elliot Sober's "The Design Argument" (in William Mann, editor, *The Blackwell Guide to the Philosophy of Religion*. Oxford: Blackwell, pp. 117–147).

4. Chicago, Illinois, outside the Adler Planetarium: The Cosmological Argument

- The classic statement of the cosmological argument can be found in Aquinas' "The Five Ways" (from his *Summa Theologica*, First Part, a, Question 2, Article 3).
- For a thorough and somewhat technical evaluation of the cosmological argument, with particular attention to the principle of sufficient reason, see Alexander R. Pruss, *The Principle of Sufficient Reason: A Reassessment* (Cambridge: Cambridge University Press, 2006).
- For a detailed discussion of the problem of how a perfect God can be free, see William Rowe's *Can God be Free?* (Oxford: Clarendon Press, 2004). Rowe engages with both the historical and the contemporary literature.
- A sophisticated debate between a theist and an atheist, which discusses contemporary cosmology and the cosmological argument, can be found in William Lane Craig and Quentin Smith's *Theism, Atheism and Big Bang Cosmology* (Oxford: Clarendon Press, 1993).

5. Chicago, Illinois, in the Hotel: The Ontological Argument

- Alvin Plantinga's *On the Nature of Necessity* (New York: Oxford University Press, 1974) is an influential book on the concept of necessity that is central to the ontological argument. Plantinga devotes Chapter 10 to that argument.
- In "The Logical Structure of Anselm's Arguments" (*The Philosophical Review*, 80, 1971, pp. 28–54), Robert M. Adams provides precise, formal presentations of Anselm's reasoning and defends it ably

against some standard objections. This article assumes familiarity with symbolic logic.

- Kant's criticism of the ontological argument appears in *The Critique of Pure Reason*, A592/B620–A614/642. His discussion of whether existence is a predicate is at A598/B626.
- For a detailed discussion of Kant's criticism, see James Van Cleve's *Problems from Kant* (New York: Oxford, 1999, pp. 187–200).
- The definitive survey of the literature surrounding the ontological argument is Graham Oppy, *Ontological Arguments and Belief in God* (New York: Cambridge, 1995). Unavoidably, it is technical.

6. Somewhere in Iowa: Religious Experience, Testimony, and Miracles

- The classic discussion of the nature of religious experiences, by one of philosophy's best writers, is William James' *The Varieties of Religious Experience* (New York: Random House, 1994; first published in 1902).
- In "Do Mystics See God?" Evan Fales argues that mystical experience provides little support for theism (in Michael L. Peterson and Raymond J. VanAaragon, editors, *Contemporary Debates in Philosophy of Religion* (Oxford: Blackwell Publishing, 2004, pp. 145-58).
- For the idea that belief in God is basic, see Alvin Plantinga's "Reason and Belief in God" (in Plantinga and Nicholas Wolterstorff, editors, *Faith and Rationality*, South Bend: University of Notre Dame Press, 1983, pp. 16–93).
- For a sophisticated defense of religious experience as a source of knowledge, see William Alston's *Perceiving God: The Epistemology of Religious Experience* (Ithaca: Cornell University Press, 1991).
- For a history of the various alterations made to the Bible, see Bart D. Ehrman's *Misquoting Jesus: The Story behind Who Changed the Bible and Why* (New York: HarperCollins, 2005).

7. Holcomb, Kansas: The Problem of Evil

- *The Problem of Evil*, edited by Marilyn M. Adams and Robert M. Adams (New York: Oxford University Press, 1990), is an excellent collection of writings on the topic. Diverse perspectives are well represented.

- J. L. Mackie's *The Miracle of Theism* (Cambridge: Oxford University Press, 1982) includes one of the clearest presentations of the problem of evil.
- Another clear, forceful presentation is "God and the Problem of Evil" (in *The Atheist Debater's Handbook,* Amherst, NY: Prometheus Books, 1983, pp. 99–108. The author's identity is unknown; it is listed as "B. C. Johnson"—a pen name.)
- John Hicks' *Evil and the God of Love* (London: MacMillan, 2007; first edition published in 1966) attempts to answer the problem of evil from a Christian perspective. Hicks' book is readable and forcefully argued.
- Another such attempt is Alvin Plantinga's short and sophisticated *God, Freedom and Evil* (New York: Harper and Row, 1974).
- A third sophisticated attempt is Richard Swinburne's *Providence and the Problem from Evil* (New York: Oxford University Press, 1998).
- For a balanced, critical discussion of the problem and the contemporary literature, see Derk Pereboom, "The Problem of Evil" (in William Mann, editor, *The Blackwell Guide to the Philosophy of Religion.* Oxford: Blackwell Publishing, pp. 148–170).
- Robert M. Adams disputes the widely help assumption that a perfect God would have to have created the best of all possible worlds, in his influential 1972 article, "Must God Create the Best?" (*The Philosophical Review, 81,* pp. 317–332; reprinted in his *The Virtue of Faith and Other Essays in Philosophical Theology*, New York: Oxford University Press, 1987).

8. Las Vegas, Nevada: Pascal's Wager

- A well-known elaboration and defense of Pascal's wager is William G. Lycan and George Schlesinger's "You Bet Your Life" (in R. Douglas Geivett and Brendan Sweetman, editors, *Contemporary Perspectives on Religious Epistemology*, New York: Oxford University Press, 1992, pp. 270–282; originally published in 1988). Lycan and Schlesinger address numerous standard objections, including the many-gods objection.
- *Gambling on God* (Lanham, MD: Rowman & Littlefield, 1994), edited by Jeff Jordan, collects recent articles on the wager. It includes a full bibliography of writings on the topic.

9. California: Faith and the Rationality of Belief in God

• In *Saving God: Religion after Idolatry* (Princeton: Princeton University Press, 2009), Mark Johnston develops a nontraditional theistic view on which God is neither separable from nature nor especially concerned with human interests.

• Christopher Hitchens' atheist manifesto, *God Is Not Great: How Religion Poisons Everything* (New York: Hachette Book Group, 2007), is, though incautious and polemical, provocative. It contains useful reflections on the costs of faith.

• Daniel C. Dennett provides a readable naturalistic treatment of religious belief in *Breaking the Spell: Religion as a Natural Phenomenon* (New York: Penguin Books, 2006). Dennett draws heavily on recent research in the cognitive sciences.

• Søren Kierkegaard presents his views on faith and reason in *Concluding Unscientific Postscript* (trans. David F. Swenson: introduction, notes, and completion of translation by Walter Lowrie; Princeton: Princeton University Press, 1941).

• Robert M. Adams provides excellent critical discussions of Kierkegaard's views in "Kierkegaard's Arguments against Objective Reasoning in Religion" (*The Monist, 60*, 1976, pp. 228–243) and "The Leap of Faith" (in Adams' *The Virtue of Faith and Other Essays in Philosophical Theology*, New York: Oxford University Press, 1987, pp. 42–47).

• In "Grammar and Religious Belief" (in Brian Davies, editor, *Philosophy of Religion* (Oxford: Oxford University Press, 2000; excerpted from "Philosophy, Theology, and the Reality of God," *The Philosophical Quarterly, 13*, 1963, pp. 108–114), D. Z. Phillips argues that religious talk does not always mean what it seems to mean, and that religious claims therefore do not require evidence in the way that empirical claims do.

• In "The Groundlessness of Religious Belief" (also in Davies, editor, *Philosophy of Religion*, pp. 115–122; excerpted from "The Groundlessness of Belief," in Stuart C. Brown, editor, *Reason and Religion*, Ithaca: Cornell University Press, 1977), Norman Malcolm argues that religious belief embodies a way of life that should not be judged as either theoretically justified or theoretically unjustified.

Sources of Quotations

Page 19: Paley, W. *Natural Theology: or Evidences of the Existence and Attributes of the Deity, Collected from the Appearances of Nature.* London: Faulder (1802), chapter 1.

Page 42: Huxley, T. H. *Lessons in Elementary Physiology.* London: The MacMillan Co. (1866), p. 193.

Pages 79–80: Anselm, *Proslogian*, chapter 2.

Page 101: *"And the angel said unto her…"* from the *Book of Luke* 1:30, King James translation.

Page 102: *"And in the fourth watch of the night…"* from the *Book of Mathew* 14:25, King James translation.

Page 116: Hume, D. *An Enquiry Concerning Human Understanding.* Indianapolis: Hackett Publishing Company (1977: originally published in 1748), p. 77.

Index